Making Summer Count

How Summer Programs Can Boost Children's Learning

JENNIFER SLOAN MCCOMBS * CATHERINE H. AUGUSTINE
HEATHER L. SCHWARTZ * SUSAN J. BODILLY * BRIAN MCINNIS
DAHLIA S. LICHTER * AMANDA BROWN CROSS

Commissioned by

The Wallace Foundation

Supporting ideas.
Sharing solutions.
Expanding opportunities.

RAND EDUCATION

The research in this report was produced within RAND Education, a unit of the RAND Corporation. The research was commissioned by The Wallace Foundation.

Library of Congress Cataloging-in-Publication Data is available for this publication.

ISBN 978-0-8330-5266-7

Cover photograph courtesy Media Bakery

Published 2011 by the RAND Corporation
1776 Main Street, P.O. Box 2138, Santa Monica, CA 90407-2138
1200 South Hayes Street, Arlington, VA 22202-5050
4570 Fifth Avenue, Suite 600, Pittsburgh, PA 15213-2665
RAND URL: http://www.rand.org/
To order RAND documents or to obtain additional information, contact
Distribution Services: Telephone: (310) 451-7002;
Fax: (310) 451-6915; Email: order@rand.org

Preface

Summer learning programs have the potential to help children and youth improve their academic and other outcomes. This is especially true for children from low-income families who might not have access to educational resources throughout the summer months and for low-achieving students who need additional time to master academic content. However, summer learning programs are often an afterthought of school districts or not offered at all, especially in restrictive funding environments.

To focus attention on the potential of such programs, this monograph reviews the literature on summer learning loss and the effectiveness of summer learning programs, determines key cost drivers of and available funds for summer programs, and gathers information about how such programs operate in district and city contexts, including facilitators and challenges.

The findings should be of interest to policymakers and practitioners involved in improving the performance of and expanding opportunities for low-income and low-achieving students, including school district and city leaders, the National Summer Learning Association, the Council of the Great City Schools, the U.S. Department of Education, funders of summer learning programs, state departments of education, state legislators, and the education research community.

This research was conducted by RAND Education, a unit of the RAND Corporation, and sponsored by The Wallace Foundation, which seeks to support and share effective ideas and practices to improve learning and enrichment opportunities for children. Its current objectives are to improve the quality of schools, primarily by developing and placing effective principals in high-need schools; improve the quality of and access to out-of-school-time programs through coordinated city systems and by strengthening the financial management skills of providers; integrate in- and out-of-school learning by supporting efforts to reimagine and expand learning time during the traditional school day and year as well as during the summer months, helping to expand access to arts learning, and using technology as a tool for teaching and promoting creativity and imagination. For more information about research on these and other related topics, please visit The Wallace Foundation Knowledge Center at www.wallacefoundation.org.

Contents

Figures

Tables

Summary

During summer vacation, many students lose knowledge and skills. By the end of summer, students perform, on average, one month behind where they left off in the spring. Of course, not all students experience "average" losses. Summer learning loss disproportionately affects low-income students. While all students lose some ground in mathematics over the summer, low-income students lose more ground in reading, while their higher-income peers may even gain. Most disturbing is that summer learning loss is cumulative; over time, the difference between the summer learning rates of low-income and higher-income students contributes substantially to the achievement gap.

Because many students lose learning over the summer and some students need more time on task to master content, participation in summer learning programs should mitigate learning loss and could even produce achievement gains. Indeed, educators and policymakers are increasingly promoting summer learning as a key strategy to improving the achievement of low-performing students. In 2009, a Johns Hopkins University–based center for summer learning became an independent organization, the National Summer Learning Association, providing resources, guidance, and expertise to the summer learning community. In 2010, President Obama noted, "Students are losing a lot of what they learn during the school year during the summer."[1] Earlier that year, First Lady Michelle Obama launched "United We Serve: Let's Read, Let's Move," a program that encourages Americans to fight the summer reading gap, acknowledging that youth who do not read during the summer can lose months of academic progress (White House, 2010).

Study Purpose and Research Questions

The Wallace Foundation is encouraging the establishment of district-supported summer learning programs, particularly for urban students in grades 1–8. To support this effort, The Foundation asked RAND to conduct a study to assess both the need

[1] The remark was made during an interview on NBC's *Today Show*, September 27, 2010.

for summer learning programs and the existing evidence on effective, viable, and sustainable summer learning programs in urban districts.

In this monograph, we address the following research questions:

1. What is the nature of summer learning loss?
2. Are summer learning programs effective in improving student achievement? What are the elements of effective summer programs?
3. How much do summer learning programs cost?
4. What are the facilitators and challenges to implementing summer programs?

Data and Methods

To answer our first two research questions, we conducted literature reviews on summer learning loss and the effectiveness of summer learning programs. To examine cost, we conducted a literature review to identify common funding sources for summer programs, collected detailed cost data from seven summer learning programs, and determined their costs and the primary reasons for the variation among them. To address the final question, regarding facilitators and challenges to implementing such programs, we conducted 15 telephone interviews: eight with providers (either school districts or programs affiliated with school districts) and seven with national nondistrict providers.

We also conducted site visits to five cities, where we interviewed summer learning leaders from among city and district representatives, summer learning staff, and external partners (more than 60 interviews in total). In four of the cities, we had the opportunity to observe summer learning. Cities selected for interviews and site visits were those that had a long history of providing summer programs or were considered by the national organizations to have particularly innovative programming or a particular context of interest, such as city-led programming or high proportions of English language learners.

Limitations and Contributions

This monograph does not include any independent analyses to determine the nature of summer learning loss or summer program effectiveness. Instead, it summarizes and draws out lessons from a set of existing research. While our independent cost analysis provides much-needed information for the field, it is limited to seven cases of academically oriented summer programming that operate at scale. Thus, it does not capture the cost range of all types of summer learning programs. In addition, because our findings and recommendations are drawn from a limited sample of summer programs that are not representative of all summer learning program contexts, they are not generalizable to all programs. In particular, by design, we spent more time studying programs provided by school districts than we did studying those provided by national or community-based summer learning providers. We also made no attempt to assess the quality of the summer programs that we visited.

Despite these limitations, this monograph makes an important contribution to the field by addressing both the value and the cost of summer learning programs. We synthesize evidence from the research about summer learning loss and the effectiveness of summer learning programs in preventing that loss. We also estimate the potential costs of such programs and provide lessons learned from districts and other providers about how to fund, implement, and sustain such programs.

Key Findings

Summer Learning Loss, Which Is Disproportionate and Cumulative, Contributes Substantially to the Achievement Gap

Research indicates that, on average, students lose skills over the summer, particularly in mathematics. However, not all students experience "average" losses, and summer learning loss disproportionately affects low-income students. Low-income students lose substantial ground in reading during the summer, while their higher-income peers often gain. Most disturbing is that it appears that summer learning loss is cumulative and that, over time, these periods of differential learning rates between low-income and higher-income students contribute substantially to the achievement gap in reading. It may be that efforts to close the achievement gap during the school year alone will be unsuccessful.

Students Who Attend Summer Programs Have Better Outcomes Than Similar Peers Who Do Not Attend These Programs

Rigorous studies of voluntary summer programs, mandatory summer programs, and programs that encourage students to read at home in the summer have all found positive effects on student achievement. The combined evidence from these studies suggests that all of these types of summer learning programs can mitigate summer learning losses and even lead to achievement gains. Moreover, longitudinal studies conclude that the effects of summer learning programs endure for at least two years after the student has engaged in the summer program. (No studies have examined whether effects last beyond two years.)

Strategies for Maximizing Quality, Enrollment, and Attendance Are Critical to Achieving Benefits

Not all summer learning programs result in positive outcomes for enrollees. Programming needs to be high-quality, and students need to enroll and attend regularly.

Research points to several practices that are associated with program quality, including individualized instruction, parental involvement, and small class sizes. For voluntary summer learning programs, providers need to adopt targeted strategies to build enrollment and maximize attendance among enrollees. Several effective strategies were offered by the program staff we interviewed. Notifying parents early before they make other plans for the summer was important in maximizing enrollment. Offering engaging enrichment activities, providing transportation, and offering full-day programs, which better suit the needs of working families, were noted as methods of increasing enrollment and encouraging high attendance rates.

Cost Is the Main Barrier to Implementing Summer Learning Programs

Providing a high-quality summer learning program can cost between $1,109 and $2,801 per child for a six-hour-per-day, five-week program. Although preliminary evidence suggests that the cost of summer school programs can be less than two-thirds of what providers spend on programs during the academic year (on a per-slot, per-week basis), summer programs nonetheless represent an additional cost to districts, especially relative to other interventions that simply update or reform practices used during the school year.

Districts Question the Cost-Effectiveness of Summer Learning Programs, and Many Have Discontinued Them in Response to Budget Cuts

Interviewees from the National Summer Learning Association indicated that, given the costs, districts are uncertain of the value they would get from a summer learning program. Furthermore, some of our interviewees who are currently offering summer learning programs questioned the extent to which the benefits of the program outweigh the costs. In fact, the recent economic downturn has created such severe shortfalls in state education budgets that many districts across the country have cut what little summer school programming they have offered. However, district leaders who are committed to such programs have found creative ways to fund them.

Partnerships Can Strengthen Summer Learning Programs

The majority of the summer learning programs examined in this study were provided by or operated in partnership with districts, and we found benefits from these partnerships. We found that summer learning programs cost less when offered by school districts due, in part, to lower central office costs and in-kind contributions of services, such as facilities and meals. In addition, districts can leverage consistent sources of funding (e.g., Title I or general operating funds) for such programs, creating a greater likelihood of sustainment. We also found that partnerships between districts and community-based organizations (CBOs) provided increased benefits and lowered costs. CBOs offered opportunities for enrichment beyond those typically offered in schools, such as kayaking and fencing, that encouraged students to enroll and attend—steps critical to program effectiveness. We also found that CBO instructors were less expensive than certified teachers. Thus, partnerships between these two types of organizations resulted in lower costs overall. Further, in one city, provision of enrichment opportunities attracted local foundation funding for summer programs.

Developing and Sustaining District-Based Voluntary Summer Learning Programs Is Challenging but Feasible

Interviewees reported that launching a summer learning program that serves a high proportion of low-performing students is challenging. Early implementation challenges include establishing consistent expectations for the program, navigating internal district bureaucracies, and partnering with local CBOs. Ongoing challenges to maintaining a summer learning program include funding (particularly during times of constrained school budgets), facilities constraints due to building maintenance or lack of air conditioning, low or uncertain enrollment, and an underspecified or unsupported vision for the summer program. Interviewees also reported that the lack of evaluations and teacher contract rules threatened the quality of their programs. Despite these challenges, some urban districts have long-standing summer learning programs, and others have launched new programs over the last few years. Challenges can be overcome by supportive leaders who can find and dedicate funding, as well as ensure that qualified staff devote time to early planning, early hiring, and early recruiting for summer learning programs.

Recommendations for Districts and Providers

Districts and communities must decide for themselves whether the potential value of these programs is worth the cost and effort of establishing and sustaining them. But our analysis suggests that they should be seriously considered within the context of the needs and resources available to districts and communities. Rigorous studies have shown that strong summer programs can achieve several important goals: reverse summer learning loss, achieve learning gains, and give low-performing students the chance to master material that they did not learn during the previous school year.

Here, we offer a set of recommendations for districts and other providers that want to invest in summer learning programs. Specifically, we recommend that districts and providers invest in staffing and planning for summer learning programs, actively incorporate practices that will help ensure the success of programs, and maximize the benefits of partnerships and a variety of funding sources.

Invest in Highly Qualified Staff and Early Planning

Developing high-quality summer programs can be challenging. We found that providers that succeeded in developing a well-structured program that attracted students to enroll and attend had high-quality, dedicated year-round administrators with time devoted to planning and programming. Planning began early in the school year. Early planning allowed programs to conduct early hiring (thereby maximizing their teacher recruiting pool) and early recruiting (thereby maximizing student enrollment).

Embed Promising Practices into Summer Learning Programs

Research shows that a number of practices are associated with improved student outcomes, such as smaller class sizes, involving parents, providing individualized instruction, and maximizing students' attendance. Other best practices include providing structures that support high-quality instruction, aligning the school year and summer curricula, including content beyond remediation, and tracking effectiveness. Providers also need to adopt strategies for attracting students to these programs to ensure value for their investment, such as print and radio advertising; advertising at community meetings, summer learning fairs, and even grocery stores; targeted recruiting of students living in housing projects, including door-to-door recruiting and phone calls to parents; student and teacher focus groups; and CBO recruiting among students in their after-school programs.

Consider Partnerships When Developing Summer Learning Programs

Partnerships may enable the creation and sustainment of high-quality voluntary summer learning programs. We found benefits from partnerships between school districts and CBOs that included a wider variety of programming options, and more varied funding sources. However, a number of other partnerships may be beneficial, as several types of organizations have an interest in promoting summer learning experiences for youth—districts, CBOs, private summer learning providers, cities, and local funders. Each of these organizations has a set of resources and skills that can help build sustainable summer learning programs. We encourage leaders to consider all local resources and build appropriate partnerships when developing these programs.

Think Creatively About Funding

There are several pots of funding from which districts can draw to support summer learning programs. Researchers have documented, for example, more than 100 programs that can support summer learning. The National Summer Learning Association provides guidelines for funding summer learning programs on its website. This monograph provides other funding ideas, such as hiring AmeriCorps students and hiring teachers who need administrative hours to serve as summer site coordinators. Partnering with local CBOs can also result in economies of scale, as noted earlier.

Recommendations for Policymakers and Funders

Finally, we offer recommendations for policymakers and funders who are interested in supporting summer learning programs: Extend the research base on the efficacy of summer learning programs and support stable funding for new and existing programs.

Extend the Research Base

Although research has established the efficacy of summer learning programs, it has not tested several aspects of such programs when offered to large numbers of low-performing students in urban settings. Rigorous, longitudinal research on large programs would provide valuable information to policymakers and practitioners. In particular, we make the following recommendations:

- Conduct randomized controlled trials of programs designed to maximize attendance that compare treated to nontreated students over multiple years.
- Conduct studies that include multiple outcomes beyond academic performance: secondary academic outcomes, such as school attendance and graduation rates, and nonacademic outcomes, such as reductions in juvenile delinquency, improved nutrition, and increases in exercise. Including a range of outcomes will help motivate other stakeholders, such as city governments, to support or fund summer learning programs.
- Conduct studies that examine whether programs can be constructed to attract high levels of participation in multiple, consecutive years of programming. If so, the studies should evaluate the effects of consecutive years of participation on a range of student outcomes.
- Conduct studies of the cost-effectiveness of summer learning programs to help district leaders and other policymakers consider how best to invest in improving education.

Support Consistent Funding Sources for Summer Learning Programs

A key obstacle to providing summer learning programs is a lack of stable funding. Policymakers at the federal, state, and local levels can work to provide funding for summer programming by specifying that existing funding targeted to high-need youth can be used for summer programming, by establishing new funding for programs, and by fundraising for summer programming. The school district officials whom we spoke with who run summer learning programs independently confirmed that funding was contingent on the support of key leaders, including the superintendent, local politicians, and local foundations.

Provide Clear Guidance Regarding the Use of Scarce Funds

District leaders described the difficulty of braiding multiple funding sources together, given the restrictions and requirements associated with each source of funds. State policymakers could support district efforts by providing clear guidance on how federal and state funds can be combined to support summer programs.

Acknowledgments

Many people helped in conducting this study and producing this monograph. We would like to thank those at The Wallace Foundation for their substantive and financial support. In particular, Edward Pauly and Ann Stone provided valuable guidance on the intellectual and analytic components of our work. Dara Rose, Richard Laine, Christine DeVita, Pam Mendels, and Lucas Held provided other substantive insights.

Representatives from school districts, mayors' offices, CBOs, and local provider organizations also contributed their time and expertise, especially on implementation issues and cost. Representatives from some of the national provider organizations were very generous with their time and expertise and contributed substantially to the study, especially in providing details on likely costs.

The document itself benefited from the input of internal and external reviewers, including Lynn Karoly and Geoffrey Borman, and from the contributions of Laura Zakaras and Lauren Skrabala, who helped prepare the final manuscript. We acknowledge their help in improving this document.

Acknowledgments

Abbreviations

21st CCLC	21st Century Community Learning Centers program
ARRA	American Recovery and Reinvestment Act
BELL	Building Educated Leaders for Life
CBO	community-based organization
CCDF	Child Care and Development Fund
CDBG	Community Development Block Grant
CPI	Consumer Price Index
CWI	Comparable Wage Index
ECLS-K	Early Childhood Longitudinal Study, Kindergarten Class
ERIC	Education Resources Information Center
FTE	full-time equivalent
OST	out-of-school time
SES	socioeconomic status
TANF	Temporary Assistance for Needy Families

CHAPTER ONE

Introduction

Policy Context

Despite steady efforts to close the large achievement gap between disadvantaged and advantaged students over the past 40 years, significant discrepancies remain. In 2009, on the National Assessment of Educational Progress, 49 percent of low-income fourth-grade students scored at the "below basic" level in reading (the lowest proficiency level) compared with 20 percent of their higher-income students. Large achievement gaps exist for mathematics as well, with 30 percent of low-income students performing at the lowest performance level compared with only 9 percent of their higher-income peers. These trends also hold in the eighth grade, where the differences are 40 percent versus 15 percent in reading and 43 percent versus 17 percent in mathematics (U.S. Department of Education, undated). Due to the inequitable proportion of low-income minority students, similarly sized achievement gaps are found between white and black children in the United States, white and Hispanic children, and native speakers and English language learners. Depending on the subject and grade level, there has been either a modest reduction or no substantive change in the achievement gap along economic or racial lines since the 1990s.

These achievement gaps are particularly troubling because they comport with subsequent inequities in educational attainment, in which students from the bottom quartile of the income distribution are more than twice as likely to drop out of high school as students from the top quartile of the distribution (National Center for Education Statistics, 2007). Failure to complete high school has significant ramifications for the individuals themselves and for society as a whole because formal schooling is an increasingly important gateway to future employment, earnings, and attendant life chances (Belfield and Levin, 2007). Some analysts believe that closing the achievement gap would do more to promote equality in the United States than any other political strategy (Jencks and Phillips, 1998).

Increasingly, educators and policymakers are considering additional learning time to be a key strategy for improving the achievement of low-performing students, many of whom are also low-income. For instance, Title I legislation specifies summer learning time as a key strategy that can be used to turn around schools. In fact, research evidence shows (1) that students' skills and knowledge often deteriorate during the summer months, and low-income students face larger losses than other students (Cooper, Charlton, et al., 2000), and (2) that low-achieving students need additional time on task to master academic content (Brown and Saks, 1986; Walberg, 1988; Ketterlin-Geller, Chard, and Fien, 2008). As a result, instruction during the summer has the potential to stop losses that might occur and to propel students toward higher achievement.

Three approaches to preventing summer learning loss are offered most often: modifying the school calendar, extending the school year, and providing summer school. Modifying the school calendar does not add instructional days to the calendar, but it redistributes days across the calendar to replace the long summer break with several shorter breaks. Unfortunately, the quality of current evidence regarding the effectiveness of modified calendars is poor (Cooper, Valentine, et al., 2003). Extending the school year would provide students with additional days of instruction. In an interview on the *Today Show*, President Obama called for a longer school year, citing the fact that U.S. students go to school, on average, a month less than students in other developed countries. He also noted that this means that "students are losing a lot of what they learn during the school year during the summer."[1]

The clear challenge to extending the school year is its cost. In addition, in cities across the country, districts that have tried to extend the school year (or modify the calendar) have met resistance from parents, employers of teenagers, and family recreation businesses. And data suggest that more time was cut away from the instructional calendar in the 2010–2011 school year as fiscal pressures forced school districts to weigh options to furlough teachers or shorten the instructional calendar. For instance, 16 of the 30 largest school districts in California reduced the number of school days to balance their budgets, and 12 districts cut instructional time by the maximum of five days (Benefield, 2010; Freedberg, 2010).

Summer programs, the focus of this monograph, are less costly than extending the school year because they are typically offered only to a subset of students. Thus, they may be more attractive to cost-conscious districts. They also provide the opportunity to give low-income students additional instruction that could help close local achievement gaps and give struggling students additional time on task so they can master material already learned by their peers.

Research Questions

As part of its interest in expanding opportunities for students to learn outside of the school day, The Wallace Foundation wants to encourage district-supported summer

---

[1] The remark was made during an interview on NBC's *Today Show*, September 27, 2010.

learning programs, particularly for urban students in grades 1–8. To support this effort, The Foundation asked RAND to conduct a study to assess both the need for summer learning programs and the existing evidence on effective, viable, and sustainable summer learning programs in urban districts. Specifically, this monograph addresses the following research questions:

1. What is the nature of summer learning loss?
2. Are summer learning programs effective in improving student achievement? What are the elements of effective summer programs?
3. How much do summer learning programs cost?
4. What are the facilitators and challenges to implementing summer programs?

Summer Learning Programs and Site Selection

Summer programs vary along a number of dimensions:

- *Instructional purpose.* Some programs serve low-performing students and provide remedial instruction, focusing on skills that students failed to master during the school year. Other programs serve both low- and higher-performing students and focus on skills that a student will encounter in the upcoming school year, to prepare students to master the material.
- *Type of provider.* Summer learning programs are offered by school districts, national providers that operate a program in multiple cities across the country, and local providers that operate only within a particular city or region.
- *Voluntary or mandatory.* Another way in which programs vary is the extent to which they are voluntary or mandatory. Voluntary programs recruit students who may or may not choose to attend. Mandatory programs are typically provided for students who are at risk of being retained in grade, as the threat of retention becomes the method of mandating program attendance. However, even mandatory programs are not strictly mandatory—parents may choose to not send their child to summer school, and the student can try to test into the next grade in the fall without having attended a summer program.
- *Dosage.* Summer learning programs typically operate for anywhere between four and eight weeks during the summer for four or five days per week. Hours of programming vary as well. All the summer learning programs described in this monograph provide half-day academic instruction in reading and/or mathematics. However, many of the programs we studied operate for a full day and also offer enrichment activities. Enrichment may be provided by regular teachers or by

community-based organizations (CBOs).[2] Some summer learning programs specifically offer enrichment activities that are intended to address the "opportunity gap," in that they provide low-income students with opportunities that are similar to those that middle- and higher-income students have during the summer.

- *Setting.* Summer learning programs operate inside and outside the classroom. The majority of summer programs discussed here are those in which students attend a summer school site that operates for a designated number of hours and weeks over the summer. These programs can be operated in schools or outside of schools (e.g., at CBOs or college campuses). Researchers have also studied reading-at-home summer interventions. These programs send or mail books home to students, appropriately matched to their reading level and interests, to read over the course of the summer. In addition, prior to the summer, teachers might provide some scaffolding that provides students with strategies to use when reading the books over the summer.

Analytic Approach

By drawing on existing literature, program cost data, and interviews with leaders of national organizations, summer learning providers, school districts, and city governments, this study examined multiple aspects of the factors that influence urban districts' student achievement (including loss and learning) during the summer. To answer our first two research questions on the extent of summer learning loss and the effectiveness of summer learning programs, we conducted literature reviews on summer learning loss and on the effectiveness of summer learning programs. To examine cost, we conducted a literature review to identify common funding sources for summer programs, collected detailed cost data from seven summer learning programs, and determined the programs' costs and the primary reasons for the variation among them. To address our fourth research question, we conducted interviews with representatives from national organizations, national providers of summer learning programs, and district officials involved in providing summer programming to understand the factors that facilitate and challenge the implementation of summer programming for urban districts' students in kindergarten through eighth grade.

Conceptual Framework

A basic conceptual framework for district-provided summer learning programs guided our study (see Figure 1.1). Given that breaks from school during the summer result in achievement loss for students and that some students need more time on task to master content, we expect that participation in summer learning programs can miti-

---

2 We define a CBO as a private or public nonprofit organization operating within the community it serves.

Figure 1.1
Conceptual Framework for District-Provided Summer Learning Programs

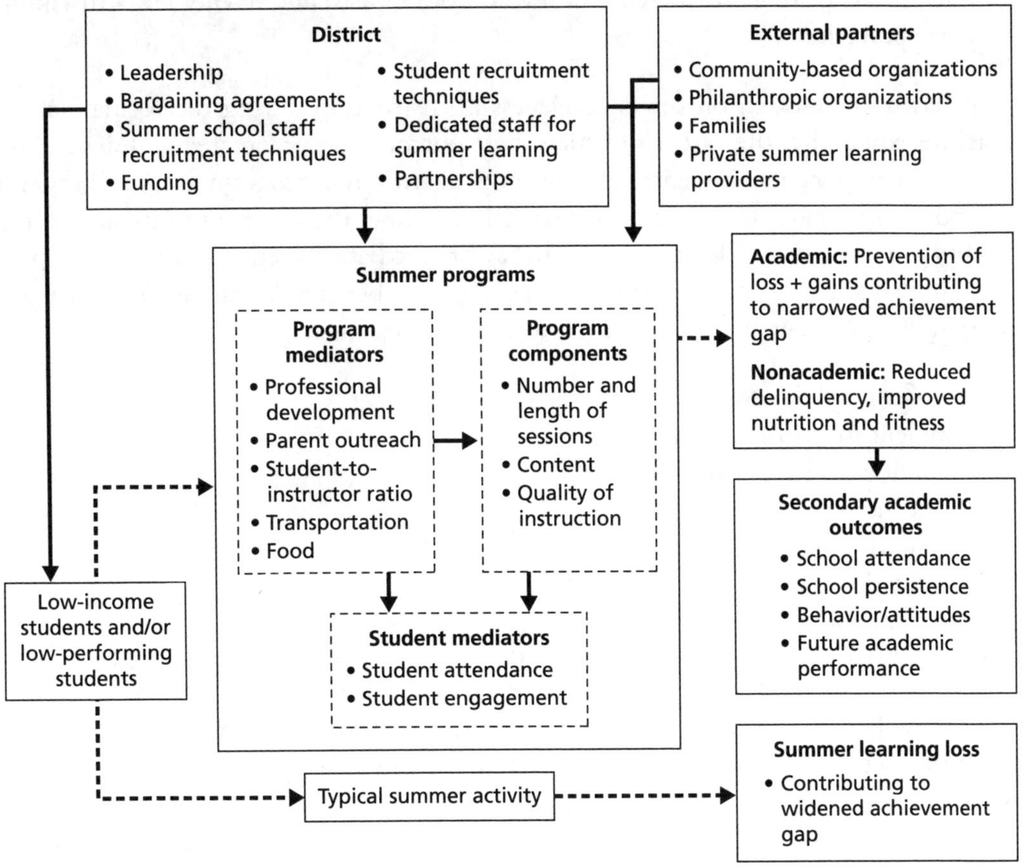

RAND *MG1120-1.1*

gate that loss and even produce achievement gains. This hypothesis is supported by prior research, described in Chapters Two and Three. By providing students with productive time on academic tasks during the summer, we expect that summer learning programs will result in improved achievement in the content areas covered by the program and will have nonacademic benefits as well. Student attendance in summer learning programs may decrease juvenile delinquency among older youth during the summer and improve students' diet and level of exercise.[3] Further, students who are better prepared academically may reap future benefits such as

- improved school-year attendance
- reduced risk of being retained in grade

[3] Researchers examining childhood obesity among kindergarten and first-grade students found that growth in body mass index is faster during the summer vacation than during the school year, especially among black and Hispanic children who are already overweight (Von Hippel et al., 2007).

- increased persistence in school, resulting in a greater likelihood of graduating
- improved socioemotional and behavioral outcomes, such as feeling more attached to school, having greater self-efficacy in subject areas, and having fewer disciplinary problems.

Based on research on the effectiveness of instruction during the regular school year, we expect that the extent to which these outcomes are generated will depend on program components, student behavior, and district and program factors. Program components include the amount of instructional time, the curriculum used, and the quality of instruction. Clearly, student behaviors mediate the effectiveness of the program in that students must be present and engaged to benefit. A number of district and program factors may also influence the quality of programs, including

- professional development
- student-to-instructor ratio
- parent engagement activities
- funding
- strength of leadership
- dedication of staff
- student and staff recruitment techniques
- use of data for program improvement.

These factors may also influence student participation and engagement. Program logistics, such as transportation and availability of food, may also influence student participation.

The ability to develop partnerships among school districts, government organizations, philanthropic organizations, CBOs, and families may affect the quality of the program as well. Each of these entities has a set of resources and skills that can build sustainable summer learning programs. Districts can offer students, teachers, student data, facilities, central office management, transportation, food services, and curricular experts. CBOs can offer deep content knowledge in certain areas and can provide enrichment opportunities that go far beyond what is typically provided in schools. Private summer learning providers have vast experience in creating engaging summer academic programs that maximize attendance. Cities can offer funds, and they have an existing interest in keeping youth safe and engaged during the summer months. Local funders can bring additional resources to these programs and can be attracted by the promise of academic and nonacademic opportunities for youth. Partnerships could maximize these resources and expertise to support quality and sustainment.

Data and Methods

Summer Learning Loss. We modeled our literature search approach after the work of Cooper, Nye, et al. (1996), using keyword searches of computerized reference databases, sifting through reference lists for relevant sources, and leveraging the expertise of education researchers who are leaders in the out-of-school-time (OST) field. Cooper, Nye, et al. (1996) provide a rigorous summary of the early evidence of summer learning loss through an extensive meta-analysis of the research published between 1975 and 1994. The literature included in Cooper, Nye, et al. (1996) was found through the computerized reference databases ERIC (Education Resources Information Center) and PsychLIT using the following keywords: summer loss, summer vacation, summer break, summer intercession, summer school, and summer variations.

We identified the work by Cooper, Nye, et al. (1996), Heyns (1978, 1987), and Entwistle and Alexander (1992) as the foundational studies on summer learning loss. We searched for studies that had referenced these pieces. Google Scholar indexed 294 publications that cited Cooper, Nye, et al. (1996); similar searches were performed for each of the other key articles. We reviewed each indexed publication citing one or more of these key articles for inclusion in our study, considering whether (1) the students represented in the research were between kindergarten and eighth grade and (2) whether summer loss was measured for an academic content area.

We also searched several computerized databases for articles published since 1994. The databases included in our search were ERIC, JSTOR, ISI Web of Knowledge, and Google Scholar. Wherever possible, we made use of "thesaurus terms," such as "summer programs," pairing them with the keywords "loss," "slide," or "gap"; ERIC identified 41, 47, and 29 publications, respectively (for a total of 117 citations). Through Google Scholar, we found 69 references that matched a search for "summer program" and "academic achievement" with the same sequence of loss-related keywords, and 23 of these references had been published between 2000 and 2010. JSTOR indexed 38 articles related to "summer loss," and the ISI Web of Knowledge was used to find 19 articles that had been published since 2000. We reviewed the abstracts to determine whether each article contained some information or assessment of summer learning loss and whether it fit our inclusion guidelines. Chapter Two presents a more detailed discussion of the extent of summer learning loss, its cumulative effects, and differences by subject and grade level.

Effectiveness of Summer Programs. We searched for rigorous studies documenting the effectiveness of summer programs. Cooper, Charlton, et al. (2000) carried out an extensive, rigorous meta-analysis of the summer learning research conducted through 1999. To be included in the analysis a program had to be provided by a school, school district, college, or university and have goals associated with preventing delinquency, improving academic performance, or improving attendance. The studies also had to compare the effects of attending versus not attending using a pre-post comparison *or* a comparison of outcomes between two groups; however, they were not required to have an experimental or quasi-experimental design. We designed our literature search to identify more recent rigorous studies.

Other articles—identified by searches of either Google Scholar or ERIC—were considered for inclusion and for further review if the summer program described in the article (1) served students between kindergarten and eighth grade, (2) measured or evaluated academic achievement, and (3) was evaluated by an external party (or had been peer-reviewed) using a quasi-experimental design (a comparison group) or a randomized controlled trial.

We found 13 studies of nine programs that met these criteria. We created a matrix to describe the range of these programs' characteristics, including academic outcomes, the evaluation method, the student population, the control group, teacher qualifications, teacher training, student recruitment, hours of instruction, attendance rates, cost, curricula, and others.

In addition to analyzing these studies for evidence on program effectiveness in general, we used Cooper, Nye, et al.'s (1996) meta-analysis findings and findings from the more recent studies to examine summer learning program effectiveness based on program components and whether or not these programs were associated with differential effects based on student characteristics. We also consulted expert opinion found in the literature, such as that provided by the U.S. Department of Education, in search of promising program characteristics. Chapter Three discusses our findings on the effectiveness of summer programs in greater detail.

Cost of Summer Programming. We consulted a variety of databases and online resources to review the literature on the financial resources required for academically oriented summer programming that targets disadvantaged children between kindergarten and eighth grade. To obtain an initial set of research documents for review, we searched four online databases: ERIC, JSTOR, ISI Web of Knowledge, and Google Scholar. In these databases we used search terms such as "summer program" or "summer school" paired with limiting terms, such as "cost," "cost-effectiveness," and sometimes "academic achievement." Using the combinations of "summer program" and "cost" and sometimes "achievement," JSTOR yielded 1,018 articles, ISI Web of Knowledge contained six articles, and ERIC offered 26 results. After excluding articles about higher education or specialized programming (such as music or outdoor education), we reviewed more than 120 abstracts to determine whether each article contained some information about the costs or sources of funds and whether it documented a program that met our criteria for full review: the given program (1) had an academic orientation and (2) served students in any grade between kindergarten and eighth. Chapter Four presents additional details on our approach to studying the cost of summer learning programs.

In addition to academic journals, we also searched the websites of leading centers, advocates, and foundations that fund either summer school programs or research. These sites included The Wallace Foundation, the William T. Grant Foundation, the

Mott Foundation, the National Summer Learning Association, Afterschool Alliance, The Finance Project, the Education Commission of the States, the Institute for Youth Education and Families, and the Harvard Family Research Project. Here, we found reports, position papers, and memos, which we retained if they met the criteria for our study. Finally, in documents that best matched our selection criteria, we also reviewed the citations to obtain further articles or other documents. Collectively, we selected 31 relevant documents as our primary sources for the literature review on the cost of summer programs.

To supplement the literature with more detailed information, we conducted semi-structured phone interviews with five school districts about their source of funds for summer programming and with seven summer school providers about the detailed costs of their programs.

The Context of Summer Learning Programs. To understand the factors that support or hinder providers' and districts' efforts to provide high-quality summer programming, during summer 2010 we conducted telephone interviews with representatives from national organizations, leaders of summer school programming in eight cities, and six national providers (see Table 1.1).

We conducted both telephone and in-person interviews. We conducted 15 telephone interviews: eight with providers (either school districts or programs affiliated with school districts) and seven with national nondistrict providers. We interviewed heads of the summer schools in the Charlotte-Mecklenburg, Cincinnati, Los Angeles, and Philadelphia school districts. We interviewed two local private providers operating in school districts—a representative from Summer Scholars, which operates several summer learning programs in the Denver Public Schools, and the executive director of

Table 1.1
Interviews, by Type

Telephone Interviews	Site-Visit Interviews	Provider Interviews	National Organization Interviews
Cincinnati, OH	Albuquerque, NM (10 individuals interviewed)	BELL (Building Educated Leaders for Life) (3 individuals interviewed)	National League of Cities
Charlotte-Mecklenburg, NC	Baltimore, MD (7 individuals interviewed)	Breakthrough Collaborative	National Summer Learning Association (3 individuals interviewed)
Dallas, TX	Minneapolis, MN (16 individuals interviewed)	Higher Achievement	
Denver, CO	Pittsburgh, PA (10 individuals interviewed)	Horizons	
Los Angeles, CA	San Francisco, CA (10 individuals interviewed)	Summer Advantage	
New Orleans, LA		Classroom, Inc.	
Philadelphia, PA			
Portland, OR			

NOTE: Unless otherwise specified, one person was interviewed at each location or organization. This list does not include those interviewed for the cost and resource portion of the study. To maintain source anonymity, discussions of cost and resource data do not identify the providers.

Big Thought, a CBO that has partnered with the Dallas Independent School District to provide summer learning opportunities for students in all grades. In New Orleans, we interviewed a representative from the Greater New Orleans Afterschool Partnership, an intermediary that coordinates out-of-school learning time across the city. In Portland, we interviewed a city leader who was serving as a coordinator for the school district and local CBOs in providing summer programming. We selected Charlotte-Mecklenburg and Los Angeles because both districts have had to cut summer learning programs for budgetary and other reasons. Including these cases deepened our perspective on the challenges that districts face in sustaining summer learning programs.

We also conducted telephone interviews with six national nondistrict providers of summer learning programs: BELL, Horizons, Breakthrough Collaborative, Higher Achievement, Classroom, Inc., and Summer Advantage. Some of these programs, like BELL, were operating in districts, and their programming was very similar to what we observed in the districts. Others, like the Breakthrough Collaborative, provide instruction primarily in nondistrict sites, such as private school settings, and have more narrow, niche programming directed toward particular types of students, such as high-performing minority students or future teachers. Although we learned quite a bit about these programs through our telephone interviews, we have more detailed information about the sites where we conducted in-person interviews.

We visited and conducted interviews at five sites that were recommended to us by summer learning practitioners and experts from the National Summer Learning Association and the National League of Cities: Albuquerque, Baltimore, Minneapolis, Pittsburgh, and San Francisco. In Baltimore, Minneapolis, and Pittsburgh, we focused on a particular summer program provided by the school district, although we also learned about other programs offered in those cities, either by the district or by other stakeholders, such as the mayor's office. For example, in Pittsburgh, we studied the Summer Dreamers Academy, a Pittsburgh Public Schools program providing summer learning opportunities for middle school students. Pittsburgh was also offering an elementary school summer program, which we did not investigate. In San Francisco, the district had lost most of its summer school funding for the 2010 summer, so we focused that visit on programming provided by CBOs and funded by the city and local foundations. At each of these sites, we interviewed school district and city administrators, summer program teachers, representatives from CBOs, funders, and others about their summer learning programs. Table 1.2 lists the sites we visited for this analysis, along with descriptive information on each.

Table 1.2
Sites Visited and Programming Types

Area of Study	Pittsburgh	Minneapolis	San Francisco	Albuquerque	Baltimore
Programs studied	Summer Dreamers Academy, which includes academic and enrichment activities offered by CBOs	Elementary and middle school summer learning program run through the district that includes academic and enrichment activities offered by CBOs	Various CBO programs funded by the city and local foundations	Elementary remedial, K–3 Plus, middle school remedial programming run by the district	New middle school program run by the district that includes academic and enrichment activities
Years of program	First year	7 years	First year without district funding and provision	K–3 Plus program in operation for the past three years; 25 years of other types of summer programming	First year
Program goal	Improving literacy and social skills; providing enrichment to address the opportunity gap	Improving academic skills and providing enrichment to address the opportunity gap	Varied goals across programs (community building, bridging the opportunity gap, and improving literacy and other academic outcomes)	Improving reading and math skills, providing a safe place and food for students in high-poverty schools	Improving middle school math skills; providing enrichment, primarily in swimming
Target population	All middle school students	High-need students in grades K–8	All students	Low-performing students in grades K–8; all K–3 students in selected high-poverty schools (K–3 Plus)	Low-performing middle school students
Number of students served	1,700	~4,000	Program enrollment and attendance vary by program	~11,000	1,200
Proportion of target population served	~30%	~50%	NA	Percentage unknown, but serving fewer students than planned and operating with many empty slots	~20%

Table 1.2—Continued

Area of Study	Pittsburgh	Minneapolis	San Francisco	Albuquerque	Baltimore
Dosage	5 days a week, 8:15 a.m.–3:00 p.m., for 5 weeks (mid-July–mid-August)	4 days a week (Monday–Thursday), 6 hours per day for five weeks	Dosage varies by program: Most programs run 5–6 weeks but Recreation and Parks programs run for 10 weeks with short intervals of different programs	Varies, with some full-day and some half-day programs	5 days a week, 5 hours a day, for 6 weeks
Cost to families	Free	Free	Free	Free	Free
Locus of control	District	District	City- and foundation-funded; CBO-run	District	District
Type of program	Remediation and "acceleration"	Remediation	Learning through enrichment	Remediation and "jump-start"	Remediation
Content	Literacy, social skills, enrichment	Varies by grade level, but all include some literacy, math, and enrichment activities through the Seeds of Science/Roots of Reading curriculum	Enrichment, some math and literacy activities	Math, literacy, some enrichment provided by teachers	Math, enrichment
Providers	Schools/teachers with enrichment through CBOs	Schools/teachers with enrichment through CBOs	CBOs	Schools/teachers	Schools/teachers and local artists, Michael Phelps's Program
Outcomes	Student gains from spring to fall on district benchmark tests, matched—but did not exceed—gains made by similar students who were not in the program	NA	NA	Beginning internal pre- and post- assessments and examination of spring and fall assessments Recently developed partnership with University of Utah for an evaluation of the K–3 Plus program	Students gained skills over the summer, but it is unclear how these gains compared to those of students not enrolled in the program

Although each site was recommended because the nominator thought it had a successful, innovative, or long-standing summer learning program, the programs varied in several ways:

- Some were brand new; others were several years old.
- While all the programs espoused academic improvement goals, other goals and concomitant target populations varied across the providers.
- Some of the programs were led by districts; others by CBOs.
- In four of the five sites we visited, the district developed and funded the summer learning program. In San Francisco, the district lost funding to support its summer learning programs (although it continued to fund some programs for high school seniors and special education students). In that case, city and private agencies stepped in and directed funding to CBOs to provide ongoing summer programming. While all providers funded by the city were required to include an academic learning component, this was not standardized across programs, and there was no requirement that the academic content be provided by licensed teachers.
- Although each of these cities' programs served at least 1,000 students, the proportion of the target population served ranged from 20 to 50 percent.
- Dosage varied across the programs, ranging from five to six hours a day, four to five days a week, and five to six weeks in total.
- These programs targeted low-performing or high-need students. However, some districts, like Pittsburgh, accepted all students who enrolled in the program, even if the curriculum was designed for lower-achieving students. Indeed, these programs are primarily remedial in focus, but two programs were also attempting to accelerate learning over the summer in an effort to jump-start students' learning in the following fall.
- Some programs employed certified teachers for academic instruction and CBO staff for enrichment programming, while Albuquerque's program was more akin to traditional "summer school" programs, with teachers (rather than CBOs) providing enrichment.
- Baltimore, Pittsburgh, and Albuquerque had evaluated their summer programs. Both the Baltimore and Pittsburgh evaluations concluded that students who participated in the program gained, but it is unclear whether they gained more than similar students who did not participate. The Pittsburgh evaluation found that low-income students in the program did not outperform low-income students who did not participate, but the study did not compare students of comparable academic backgrounds. The results of the Albuquerque study were not yet available as of this writing.

We interviewed participants using semistructured interview protocols that were developed to match the study's conceptual framework. Topics included structure, content, curriculum, instructional methods, professional development, average student attendance, recruiting methods, parental involvement strategies, funding, teacher hiring practices, external partnerships, and facilitators and challenges.

Researchers' notes were used to develop summaries of each program, organized according to a common template. We analyzed these templates both structurally and thematically. Our structural analysis compared answers to the same questions across sites to systematically compare programs' components, strategies, practices, facilitators, and challenges.

We also conducted thematic analyses, looking across all answers to our questions for themes related to our conceptual framework, such as on the topics of funding and quality. We also noted instances of unique, promising practices and of disconfirming evidence (e.g., where findings did not align with the conceptual framework).

Study Limitations

This study relied on prior research to describe the nature of summer loss and summer program effectiveness. While our independent cost analysis provides much-needed information for the field, it is limited to seven cases, which do not represent the full range of costs across all summer learning programs. We selected academically oriented summer programs that operate at scale for our cost analysis. In addition, our findings and recommendations are drawn from a limited sample of summer programs, and the programs included, by design, are primarily run by or in partnership with school districts. Thus, these data are not representative of all summer learning program contexts, nor are the findings generalizable to all programs.

Our study did not attempt to judge the quality of the summer programs examined. Nor did it attempt to count the number of summer learning programs offered in urban districts across the country. We were told by representatives from the National Summer Learning Association that many urban districts provide programs for a subset of their populations (e.g., English language learners, high school students in need of credit recovery, special education students), but large-scale programs offering comprehensive summer learning opportunities that target all low-performing or low-income students are rare. Indeed, the National Summer Learning Association website references 69 "member organizations and districts"; only three are school districts and none are large, urban districts (see National Summer Learning Association, undated[a]). We therefore conclude that district-based, large-scale summer learning programs are not ubiquitous in urban districts, but we found no data to confirm this assumption.

Despite these limitations, this monograph contributes to the literature in that it builds a broad conceptual framework for summer learning, drawing together information on the nature of summer loss, expectations for summer learning program effectiveness, the range of potential costs and the identification of cost drivers, and evidence on how districts and providers implement and maintain programs.

Organization of This Monograph

The next two chapters synthesize the evidence in the research on the value of summer learning programs. In Chapter Two, we review the findings on summer learning loss, beginning with an overview of research on the connection between time and learning and learning decay, then focusing specifically on evidence of summer learning losses in mathematics and reading. In Chapter Three, we focus on the effects of summer learning programs on achievement, including overall effects, effects over time, and the differences in these effects as they relate to student demographics, grade level, and attendance. We also summarize the literature on recommended practices for summer programming. Chapters Four and Five address key obstacles that districts face in developing summer learning programs: cost (Chapter Four) and the challenge of implementing, sustaining, and scaling high-quality programs (Chapter Five). Chapter Six concludes with a discussion of the findings and recommendations for practitioners and policymakers.

[illegible]

Organization of This Monograph

[illegible]

CHAPTER TWO

Time, Learning, Learning Decay, and Summer Learning Loss

In this chapter, we explore the nature of summer learning loss and its effects. We first provide some background on the relationship between time and learning to create the conceptual link between summer vacation and loss of academic skills. Many of the findings in this chapter are derived from Cooper, Nye, et al.'s 1996 analysis of the literature on summer learning loss. In addition, we draw heavily on two key longitudinal studies conducted in Atlanta and Baltimore, which tracked students over time and enabled an examination of the effects of school separately from the effects of summer and the impact of summer learning loss over time. We also highlight the extent to which summer learning loss has been found to differ according to student characteristics, grade level, and subject.

General Relationship Between Time and Learning

The phenomenon of adult learning, retention, and relearning was investigated heavily from the 1950s through the 1980s in noneducation fields, such as the military and industrial sectors. The military, in particular, was interested in what training its recruits would remember after a period of nonpractice and how often their skill acquisition would need refreshing. This large body of literature led to the following conclusions, based on adult learning of specific tasks (Naylor and Briggs, 1961; Adams, 1967; Garlin and Sitterley, 1972; Baldwin, Cliborn, and Foskett, 1976; Prophet, 1977; Schendel, Shields, and Katz, 1978; Osborn, Campbell, and Harris, 1979; Shields, Goldberg, and Dressel, 1979; Hagman, 1980; Goldberg, Drillings, and Dressel, 1981; and Schendel and Hagman, 1982). The following findings were of significance for our study:

- In the absence of practice or other reinforcement, skills deteriorate over time at a rate that is initially quite rapid, with the rate of decay slowing over time.
- The rate of decay varies by task or skill. Tasks with performance that deteriorates rapidly tend to be procedural, involve a number of steps, have no performance

cues, or have no time requirements. Task performance decays more slowly for tasks that are continuous, with cues or obvious internal logic.
- The best predictor of the rate of decay for a task is the individual's original level of learning. The higher the level of proficiency before a nonpractice period, the greater the retention.
- The training method that produces the highest initial learning and performance will produce the best retention over time.
- The time needed to relearn tasks is less than the time needed to originally learn them.

Time and Learning in and out of School

Simultaneously, the connection between school learning and time was also being investigated. Carroll (1963, 1989) is credited with proposing perhaps the most influential conceptual model that others have used to launch investigations into time and learning in school settings. In his conceptualization, based on studies of foreign language acquisition, students bring three attributes to school learning: aptitude, perseverance, and ability to comprehend. Aptitude is the amount of time a specific student needs to master a learning objective. Students with high aptitude will learn the objective more quickly than those with low aptitude. Perseverance is the amount of time a student is willing to invest in mastering the objective. Some students, through interest or through learned discipline, spend more time learning. The ability to comprehend the instruction is generally related to language comprehension and the ability to understand the learning task. Carroll's conceptualization also included two major constructs influenced by the school and classroom teacher: opportunity to learn and quality of instruction. The former is the time allotted for learning a construct, and the latter is the organization of the instruction for ease of acquisition for the specific student. Carroll did not elaborate further on instructional quality but included the notions that students must be clearly told what the learning goal is, that they must be provided with learning materials, and that steps in learning must be well planned and organized.

Later work in this field focused on adding constructs to the theory and delving into the specific drivers of the individual learning components and their relationships with one other. The Beginning Teacher Evaluation Study, a groundbreaking study in the 1970s by Charles Fisher and David Berliner, found that students had to be engaged and that instruction had to be appropriate for the student's level to create a strong relationship between learning time and student achievement gains (Fisher et al., 1980). Other studies have referred to this combination of time, engagement, and appropriate level of instruction as academic learning time. Lomax's review of time-on-task research in the 1970s supports the relationship between academic learning time and student achievement (Lomax and Cooley, 1979), as does research from the 1980s by Karweit and Slavin (1982). Research through the 1990s (Cotton, 1989; Aronson, Zimmerman, and Carlos, 1998) showed little or no relationship between allocated time and student achievement, some relationship between instructional time and student achievement, and a larger relationship between academic learning time and student achievement. However, research in the late 1980s and 1990s began to question the theoretical model correlating academic learning time and student achievement gains, claiming that it is important to take into consideration the different rates at which students learn (Gettinger, 1989). In general, key concepts and findings emerging from this work include the following:

- Manipulating the time spent on learning and/or increasing the quality of instruction ensures that almost all students can learn at higher levels (Bloom, 1976).
- Researchers generally distinguish between allocated time (the time on the school calendar for a given content area) and academic learning time (the amount of time students spend working on rigorous tasks at the appropriate level of difficulty). Academic learning time is more predictive of student achievement (Harnischfeger and Wiley, 1976; Lomax and Cooley, 1979; Fisher et al., 1980; Karweit and Slavin, 1982; Hawley et al., 1984; and Karweit, 1985).
- Spaced practice (once a day for several days) as opposed to one long, concentrated lesson (all day long for just one day) appears to be more effective in facilitating learning (Walberg, 1988; Rohrer and Taylor, 2006; Rohrer and Pashler, 2010). In addition, more practice does not necessarily improve retention of learned material: Fewer problems spaced over at least one week should lead to greater retention than would more problems completed in a shorter duration (Rohrer and Taylor, 2006).
- Students with lower achievement will learn at slower rates than those who start at a higher level of achievement (Walberg, 1988), and there is some evidence that low-performing students, in particular, benefit from more time on task (Brown and Saks, 1986; Ketterlin-Geller, Chard, and Fien, 2008).
- Factors outside of school affect time spent learning, including the home environment, peer influences outside the school, and TV-watching habits (Haertel, Walberg, and Weinstein, 1983).

Past research has established a link between relevant academic learning time and student achievement. Although instructional time, in and of itself, is not sufficient, it is necessary in order to provide the relevant academic learning time. Compared to other developed countries, students in the United States receive fewer hours of instruction—799 per year compared with 861 in Finland, 911 in the Netherlands, 928 in Japan, and 1,079 in Korea (Silva, 2007). Furthermore, the American school calendar is notable for its long, formal summer break, especially when compared to school calendars in other countries. Some countries have shorter, more equally spaced breaks, while others have formal mechanisms to help students retain over breaks what they learned in school (Wiseman and Baker, 2004).

Summer Learning Loss

The typical U.S. student goes to school for nine months out of the year and experiences a three-month summer vacation. Given that learning can decay, it is not surprising that many students experience summer learning loss. In this section, we describe the overall findings regarding summer learning loss and whether the extent of summer learning loss differs by student characteristics, is cumulative over time, or differs by grade or subject.

Average Summer Loss of Learning

Cooper, Nye, et al. (1996) conducted a meta-analysis of 13 studies of summer learning loss that focused on grades 1–9. This analysis provides rigorous estimates of summer learning loss, at least for those grades and for most children. Cooper and his colleagues found that the average student score in the fall is about one-tenth of a standard deviation below the spring average. They assume nine to ten months of school per year and note an effect size of 0.10, indicating that summer learning loss equates to approximately one month of instruction. However, this varies by grade level, as found by Hill et al. (2007; see Table 2.1).[1] Thus, upon returning to school in the fall students performed, on average, roughly one month behind where they performed in the spring. However, research shows that not all students experience "average" losses—some post significant losses while others may even experience gains.

Many of the studies measured summer loss using existing state or district exams taken in the spring and fall. Because of this, the length of time between the pre-test and the post-test can vary, and the pre-post interval often includes significant time in classroom learning environments. This means that the difference among findings in relative gains or losses could be a function of the time interval and how much schooling occurred during the pre-post interval. Cooper, Nye, et al. (1996) performed an analysis to take this into account, using the pre-post interval as an independent variable. They showed that the longer the interval between pre- and post-testing, the lower the level of loss (because students had received benefits from school); the shorter the interval, the greater the loss (because it measured summer loss more accurately).

---

[1] Effect sizes describe the magnitude of an effect using a standardized measure. An effect size of means is the difference between two means divided by their pooled standard deviation. Translating effect sizes into months of learning is problematic unless the measure is designed to assess annual student growth.

Table 2.1
Average Annual Gains in Effect Size from Nationally Normed Tests, by Grade

	Reading Tests		Math Tests	
Grade Transition	**Mean**	**Margin of Error**	**Mean**	**Margin of Error**
K–1	1.52	±0.15	1.14	±0.22
1–2	0.97	±0.08	1.03	±0.11
2–3	0.60	±0.08	0.89	±0.12
3–4	0.36	±0.09	0.52	±0.11
4–5	0.40	±0.05	0.56	±0.08
5–6	0.32	±0.09	0.41	±0.06
6–7	0.23	±0.09	0.30	±0.05
7–8	0.26	±0.03	0.32	±0.03
8–9	0.24	±0.08	0.22	±0.08
9–10	0.19	±0.06	0.25	±0.05
10–11	0.19	±0.14	0.14	±0.12
11–12	0.06	±0.09	0.01	±0.11

SOURCE: Hill et al., 2007, p. 3, Table 1. Used with permission.

NOTE: The table shows average annual gains in effect sizes. These estimates provide an expectation for annual growth in absence of an intervention by grade transition (e.g., for grades 1–2). It demonstrates the importance of interpreting a study's effect size in relation to grade and subject.

Differences by Family Income

Research demonstrates that there are clear differences in the summer learning rates of low-income and higher-income students. Work by Heyns (1978, 1987) articulated the influence of summer learning loss on the achievement gap. It noted that comparing the school year to summer break provides an opportunity to isolate the effects of non-school influences on a young person's intellectual development. Heyns longitudinally studied fifth, sixth, and seventh graders in 42 Atlanta schools and found that the differential learning rate between white, economically advantaged students and minority, economically disadvantaged students increased during the summer, especially in reading skills (Heyns, 1978).

Similarly, using a rich set of data from a study in Baltimore, which tested students in the fall and spring in grades 1–6 and again in the spring of grade 9, Entwisle and Alexander (1992, 1994) found similar relationships for reading achievement. They concluded that low-income and higher-income students learn at nearly the same rate while in school, but during the summer, low-income students' learning falls far below that of their higher-income peers. They hypothesized that the nonschool environment of low-income students does not support educational growth to the same extent as it does for students with higher family income levels.

Cooper, Nye, et al.'s (1996) meta-analysis confirms these findings for reading. Specifically, it found that family income made a difference in absolute and relative gains and losses during the summer, and this was especially true for reading; analyses showed a three-month difference in learning in reading skills between middle-income and lower-income children over the summer. Children from lower-income families lost, on average, more learning specifically in reading comprehension and word recognition than children from higher-income families (who, in fact, made gains in word recognition).

More recent analyses of Early Childhood Longitudinal Study, Kindergarten Class (ECLS-K), data similarly suggest that some of the achievement gap between early elementary students from high- and low-income families is attributable to different learning rates over the summer months (Burkam et al., 2004; Downey, von Hippel, and Broh, 2004; Benson and Borman, 2010). Results in reading show that middle-income students maintained achievement levels over the summer while high-income students improved and low-income students lost ground (Benson and Borman, 2010). In addition, Benson and Borman found neighborhood effects whereby students from high-income neighborhoods had stronger reading growth than others.

These findings are consistent with research showing that families and factors outside of school influence reading achievement. Benson and Borman (2010) also found that low-income students entered school performing roughly one standard deviation below their higher-income peers. Low-income parents read with, teach, and talk to their children less frequently, each of which contributes to children's literacy skills and school readiness (Brooks-Gunn and Duncan, 1997). A study that used audio recordings of family interactions over the course of two years to measure language use found that children growing up in low-income families heard approximately one-half to one-third as many spoken words as children in more affluent households. Based on hour-long recordings of 42 families taken over two and a half years, Hart and Risley (1995) found that children who were born into homes with fewer economic resources learned fewer words, had fewer experiences with words in interactions with other people, and acquired a vocabulary of words more slowly than children in more affluent families. Examining these children at third grade (ages 9–10), Hart and Risley found that the amount of talk and vocabulary growth and the style of language interaction with parents at age 3 highly correlated with the students' achievement on school-oriented tests of vocabulary, listening, speaking, semantics, and syntax.

Cumulative Effects of Summer Learning Loss

Research also suggests that summer learning loss is cumulative. Given that low-income students are more likely to forget what they have learned, particularly in reading, than their higher-income peers (who can gain knowledge and skills in certain reading areas during the summer months), repeated episodes of loss result in low-income students falling further and further behind their more affluent peers. Using data from a study in Baltimore, which tracked students to age 22, Alexander, Entwisle, and Olson (2007) estimated that, over the course of the first four summers of school, the difference between summer gains by students of high and low socioeconomic status (SES) is greater than the initial difference between the groups upon school entry. The authors also estimated that approximately two-thirds of the reading achievement gap by ninth grade could be attributed to summer learning loss in the first five years of schooling.[2] However, their study included some caveats. It was a local study, and the complete sample of data included just over 300 students. The authors described results as suggestive, noting that "the detailed percentages and probabilities reported should not be generalized." However, summer learning loss is very likely cumulative; thus, over time, it contributes to a substantial portion of the achievement gap between low-income and high-income students.

Alexander, Entwisle, and Olson (2007) tracked students' educational careers further, and the achievement gap found in ninth grade was highly associated with later dropping out and whether a student took college preparatory courses. According to the authors,

> What might not have been expected is the extent to which the continuing press of school-age children's family and neighborhood environments contributes to the year 9 achievement differential between high and low SES youth: summer shortfall over the five years of elementary school accounts for more than half the difference, a larger component than that built up over the preschool years. And too, these learning differences from the early years that present themselves in 9th grade reverberate to constrain later high school curriculum placements, high school dropout, and college attendances. (Alexander, Entwisle, and Olson, 2007, p. 175)

Differences by Subject and Grade Level

In general, students are more likely to forget what they have learned in mathematics over the summer than they are to lose literacy skills. Cooper, Nye, et al. (1996) found that summer learning loss was greater, on average, for mathematics than for reading. This loss in mathematics ability was consistent across other factors, such as a student's family income and race. A number of studies have found that school quality has a greater effect on mathematics than reading because mathematics instruction occurs mostly in schools (Murnane, 1975; Bryk and Raudenbush, 1988; Allinder et al., 1992). Reading levels might be affected by factors outside of school more so than mathematics levels because families are more likely to promote and practice literacy

---

2 The authors note that the results for mathematics are similar to those found for reading, but they do not present mathematics results.

skills than mathematics skills at home (Harris and Sass, 2009). Additionally, mathematics involves fact acquisition and procedural knowledge, much like spelling skills, which are more likely to be forgotten and decay over time if not practiced (Cooper and Sweller, 1987; Geary, 1995). Since mathematics is learned primarily in schools from teachers, lack of exposure to mathematics instruction over the summer would account for the loss identified for most students.

However, analyses using the ECLS-K data, which examined summer learning loss between kindergarten and first grade, provide contrary evidence to Cooper, Nye, et al.'s finding on mathematics losses. One such study found differential rates of mathematics learning over the summer, with higher-income students showing higher gains in mathematics than lower-income students (Burkam et al., 2004). The authors noted that this result might be a phenomenon associated with the early grade levels they were studying rather than an effect that is generalizable to higher grades.

Indeed, there seem to be differences by grade level in summer learning loss among students. The meta-analysis by Cooper, Nye, et al. (1996) found that grade level was related to changes in reading achievement. As the grade level went up, the effect of summer vacation changed from positive to negative and grew more detrimental. They found that, on average, first and second graders showed nonsignificant gains in achievement, while students in fourth grade and beyond showed significant losses, "some of which were quite dramatic" (p. 263).

It is possible that the skills tested in these early grades are far more constrained (and are eventually mastered by all students), while the skills tested in later grades are far less constrained, leading to greater variation in outcomes (Paris, 2005). Cooper, Nye, et al. (1996) concluded that the negative and linear influence of increased grade level on the effect of summer vacation might be the result of a "floor effect" in scaling. They explained that, by definition, a student in the first grade can only achieve one grade below the national normed grade level, thus constraining the amount of negative change among students in earlier grades. Thus, it is important to consider the grade levels studied when interpreting findings from summer learning studies.

Conclusions

Research indicates that summer vacation may have detrimental learning effects for many students. On average, all students lose skills, particularly in mathematics. However, summer learning loss disproportionately affects low-income students, particularly in reading. While their higher-income peers, on average, post gains in reading, low-income students show losses at the end of the summer. Most disturbing is that it appears that summer learning loss is cumulative and that, over time, these periods of differential learning rates between low-income and higher-income students contribute substantially to the achievement gap. It may be that efforts to close the achievement gap during the school year alone will be unsuccessful.

Given the established connection between academic learning time and achievement and the findings regarding summer learning loss—which is particularly acute for low-income students—it is reasonable to assume that a structured program of summer instruction could help mitigate this loss. It might even produce gains.

In addition, the general learning literature indicates that low-achieving students need more time to master material and that spacing learning out over time is an effective instructional technique. Summer programs would provide these students with this additional, spaced, time. If Bloom (1976) is correct (i.e., that almost all students can master material if given enough time and proper instruction), summer learning programs might be a key strategy for improving the academic performance of struggling students. The next chapter examines the extent to which such programs have been found to be effective.

CHAPTER THREE

Effectiveness of Summer Learning Programs

This chapter reviews the existing literature on the effectiveness of summer learning programs. It draws on evidence from a meta-analysis conducted by Cooper, Charlton, et al. (2000) and from 13 experimental or quasi-experimental research studies since 2000.[1] Using evidence from these studies, we describe the overall effects of summer learning programs, effects over time, and the extent to which studies have found differential effects based on subject, student demographics, grade level, and attendance. The summer learning programs examined in the literature included voluntary at-home summer reading programs, voluntary classroom-based summer programs, and "mandatory" summer programs that students must attend to avoid retention in grade. We then discuss the characteristics of effective summer learning programs, identified by prior research and expert opinion, and conclude with implications for future summer learning programming.

Effectiveness of Summer Learning Programs

Overall Effectiveness

Prior research indicates that summer learning programs can be effective in improving student achievement. The most commonly cited measure of the overall effectiveness of summer learning programs comes from the meta-analysis conducted by Cooper, Charlton, et al. (2000). They found that effect sizes for remedial summer programs varied from –0.24 to 1.50,[2] with an average weighted effect size across the programs of +0.2 (p. 52).[3] However, when the authors restricted the analysis to the four studies that used a random assignment of students, they found that the average benefit was smaller (effect size of +0.14) but still exceeded the estimate of average summer loss.

1 While Cooper, Charlton, et al. (2000) included four studies using random assignment, they were dissertations or theses and not published in peer-reviewed journals.

2 Per Cooper, Charlton, et al. (2000), the upper bound excludes three extreme values taken from one study.

3 The average weighted d-index reported by Cooper, Charlton, et al. (2000) was +0.26. The unweighted average was +0.32, and the unweighted median effect size was +0.19.

We investigated the extent to which recent quasi-experimental and experimental studies confirmed or disconfirmed these findings and could add to our understanding of factors that influence effectiveness. We identified 13 experimental or quasi-experimental studies of nine summer learning programs published since 2000. The programs studied included voluntary classroom-based, mandatory, and at-home programs, and, in general, the studies found effect sizes that were more in line with Cooper, Charlton, et al.'s (2000) estimate from the random assignment studies. Some of the programs targeted the early primary grades (K–2), while others were for upper-elementary students. The student populations targeted by the programs varied and included students at risk of retention, low-income students, students in districts with high proportions of low-income and minority students, and all students in a district.

Three studies of mandatory remedial classroom-based programs in three school districts have concluded that the programs were effective (Jacob and Lefgren, 2004; Matsudaira, 2008; McCombs, Kirby, and Mariano, 2009), at least in the near term. Studies of voluntary elementary programs also found positive effects from summer programs (Schacter and Jo, 2005; Borman, Benson, and Overman, 2005; Chaplin and Capizzano, 2006; Borman, Goetz, and Dowling, 2009). Recent studies of reading-at-home programs using randomized controlled trial designs have also found promising or significant short-term effects (James Kim, 2006; Kim and White, 2008; Allington et al., 2010) and cumulative effects over time (Allington et al., 2010). However, other studies found no overall effects among students who were part of the treatment group (Jimmy Kim, 2004; Borman, Goetz, and Dowling, 2009; Kim and Guryan, 2010). We interpret the combined evidence from these studies, along with Cooper, Charlton, et al.'s (2000) meta-analysis, to suggest that many types of summer learning programs have the potential to reduce summer learning losses, but they are not guaranteed to do so. We now describe factors that influence the effectiveness of summer learning programs.

Subject

In their meta-analysis, Cooper, Charlton, et al. (2000) found that summer programs led to more favorable outcomes on mathematics assessments than on reading assessments. Studies of the mandatory summer programs also found higher effect sizes in mathematics than in reading, but these differences tended to be relatively small (Jacob and Lefgren, 2004; Matsudaira, 2008; McCombs, Kirby, and Mariano, 2009). However, these results might also be due to the nature of the assessments used. Hill et al. (2007) found that, for the elementary grades, the average annual gain on nationally normed tests (measured in terms of effect size) was greater in mathematics than in reading.

Demographic Groups

There are no clear, consistent results in terms of differences by demographics. Cooper, Charlton, et al.'s (2000) analyses found that remedial summer programs resulted in substantially greater gains for middle-income students compared with low-income students. This finding appears to conflict with research that has found no difference in the learning rates between low- and higher-income students during the school year (e.g., Alexander, Entwisle, and Olson, 2001). If receiving instruction acts as an equalizer during the school year, it is unclear why it would not do so during summer school programming. One possible hypothesis is that middle- and higher-income students, but not low-income students, receive additional benefits from their families. Summer school programs do not operate over the entire summer, and some operate only for half-days. Thus, family influences on achievement may be greater during the summer than during the school year. Another hypothesis is that low-income students do not attend as much as their peers from more affluent families.

Studies of programs that provide books to read at home show differences by demographic group. James Kim (2006) found a larger treatment effect for black students than for all students. Similarly, Allington et al. (2010) found the largest effects for economically disadvantaged students. It could be that, for these students, receiving books at home differed more significantly from the "status quo" than was the case for other students. However, Kim and Guryan (2010) found that the reading-at-home program was not effective in a district populated predominately by English language learners, which may imply the need to alternate strategies for reaching and advancing the summer learning of English language learners and for involving their families in this effort.

Grade

Findings regarding whether summer learning programs are more effective for one age group over another are mixed. In their meta-analysis, Cooper, Charlton, et al. (2000) found that summer programs had more positive effects for early primary and secondary grades compared to late primary grades. However, in studies that examined the effectiveness of the same summer program for multiple grade levels, findings differed. In his examination of the effects of a mandatory summer school program in an urban district, Matsudaira (2008) found that students in higher grades (late primary, in Cooper, Charlton, et al.'s analysis) benefited more from summer school than students in third grade. The studies of mandatory summer programming in Chicago (Roderick, Engel, and Nagaoka, 2003; Jacob and Lefgren, 2004) and New York City (McCombs, Kirby, and Mariano, 2009) included multiple grades but did not identify significant differences between grades.

Attendance

Studies that examined the link between outcomes and attendance found that increased attendance improves outcomes. In a study of New York City's fifth-grade mandatory remediation program, the authors found a threshold effect for mathematics under which students who had attended seven to 14 sessions outperformed their peers who had attended fewer than seven sessions (McCombs, Kirby, and Mariano, 2009, Chapter Eight).

Compelling evidence regarding the influence of attendance on outcomes comes from studies of a randomized controlled trial of a voluntary summer program offered over three summers to randomly selected kindergarten and first-grade students in ten Baltimore schools. Borman, Benson, and Overman (2005) found that the experimental effect of offering the program to certain students had no effect on reading achievement. However, each additional week of attendance in the program was associated with a 0.05 standard deviation increase in fall test scores. Analyzing the same data, Borman and Dowling (2006) reported positive effects only for those children who participated for at least two summers with attendance rates of greater than 39 percent. Students who participated less frequently did not outperform their peers who were not assigned to the treatment group. The results of this experiment highlight a key challenge facing voluntary programs: incentivizing attendance so that students will benefit from programming. Programs that seek to engage students for consecutive years face the additional challenge of incentivizing attendance across multiple years.

A recent study evaluating the effects of a three-year self-selected books-at-home intervention found strong, positive effects accrued to participants by the end of the three years (Allington et al., 2010).

Although all of these studies focused on reading, their findings hold promise for the benefits of consecutive years of participation in summer learning in general.

Long-Term Effects

We did not identify any study that examined the effectiveness of summer learning programs over the long term. None of the studies in Cooper, Charlton, et al.'s (2000) meta-analysis tracked the effects of summer school over time; thus, the authors were unable to conclude whether or not gains from summer programs persist. However, a handful of studies have examined whether effectiveness persists for one to two years after participation. The three studies of mandatory summer programs for students at risk of being retained in grade studied outcomes for students either one or two years beyond receiving summer instruction. Each of these studies examined the effect of summer programming on state assessment outcomes and found gains for participants relative to comparison students, though none of the studies tracked whether the summer program resulted in eventual proficiency (a reported goal of superintendents, as discussed in Chapter Five).

Matsudaira (2008) examined the effects of a summer program in an unnamed large, urban school district on the following year's assessment performance. He found an average positive effect for both mathematics and reading achievement the following spring. Jacob and Lefgren (2004) and Roderick, Engel, and Nagaoka (2003) studied the effects of the Chicago Public School's Summer Bridge Program and found that positive effects persisted for two years after the summer program. However, Summer Bridge did not change the learning trajectory of students during the school year. Similarly, McCombs, Kirby, and Mariano (2009) investigated the impact of New York City's fifth-grade mandatory summer learning program and found that attendance had small, positive effects that persisted into the seventh grade. While these studies identified short-term, persistent effects, none estimated whether there was any decay of effects over the longer term.

Schacter and Jo (2005) studied the effects of a first-grade summer learning program immediately after summer school and at three, six, and nine months after the intervention for decoding and reading comprehension. They found that effect sizes for decoding were strongest at the first post-test (0.96), positive but reduced at the second (0.59), and insignificant at the nine-month post-test. The intervention had strong effects for comprehension at the first post-test (1.35); the effects were significant at the second post-test (1.25) as well, but they were smaller—though still relatively large—at the final post-test (0.47). The authors hypothesized that the decline in effects might be associated with reteaching decoding skills to the nontreated students or ineffective teaching during the school year.[4]

Another hypothesis for this type of decline derives from the work of Scott Paris (2005). Paris explained that some reading skills are more constrained than others. In other words, some skills are learned quickly, mastered entirely, and thus should not be conceptualized as having enduring individual differences. For instance, all students will eventually learn the letter and sound relations for lower- and uppercase letters. This is a constrained skill—the number of elements to be mastered is small and finite. Other skills, such as comprehension, are unconstrained: Individuals can continue to further master and enhance these skills over a long period. Treating constrained skills as unconstrained in longitudinal measurement can lead to a number of erroneous interpretations, including seeing transient effects of interventions that accelerate constrained skills. It could be that the decay of the intervention effect for decoding, a relatively constrained skill set, is due in part to the general mastery of this skill by all stu-

[4] Schacter and Jo (2005) suggest that the time teachers may have spent during the fall reteaching decoding skills, in which the treatment (intervention) students may have already been proficient, may have augmented the abilities of the control students prior to the fall assessments. (The post-tests included the Gates-MacGinitie, which was administered in September and December 2001 and the Stanford Achievement Test, version 9, which was administered in May 2002.) This augmentation may explain the diminished advantage of intervention students' comprehension scores over those of the control population.

dents in the second grade. Prior research has found that the greatest rate of progress for decoding is made in second grade, the year of the post-testing (Aarnoutse et al., 2001).

Nonacademic Outcomes

We identified only one study that examined the relationship between a summer program and nonacademic outcomes. An evaluation of Building Educated Leaders for Life (BELL) found positive effects on the degree to which parents encouraged their children to read, but it found no influence on students' academic self-perceptions or social behaviors (Chaplin and Capizzano, 2006). Our conceptual framework hypothesizes that secondary nonacademic outcomes may result from improved achievement due to the program, but not directly from the program itself. No studies have examined this hypothesis.

Components of Quality Summer Learning Programs

One key question is whether the structural components of the programs, such as the duration, nature of the curricula, and teacher characteristics, contribute to different outcomes. Here, we explore the available literature on the components of high-quality programs. Some of these suggestions emerged from the research literature while others were drawn from expert opinion.

Smaller Class Sizes

Smaller class size is thought to provide teachers with more time to work individually with students and to create greater opportunities to differentiate instruction based on student needs. Research has found that small class size is associated with program effectiveness. Cooper, Charlton, et al. (2000) found that programs in which class size was capped at 20 students were more effective in producing achievement gains.

Differentiated Instruction

Summer programs that intended to provide individualized instruction were more effective than programs without this intention (Cooper, Charlton, et al., 2000). Similarly, research and experts recommend that teachers work with small learning groups (Boss and Railsback, 2002; Beckett, 2008). Differentiated or individualized instruction is an intended component in many classrooms; however, it is often difficult for teachers to implement. When faced with large class sizes and a broad range of ability levels, differentiation is a challenge. Summer programs with smaller class sizes should provide an opportunity for teachers to offer more individualized instruction to students.

High-Quality Instruction

As during the regular school year, instructional quality is directly related to improved achievement. In efforts to ensure high-quality instruction, experts recommend providing professional development to teachers (Bell and Carrillo, 2007; Boss and Railsback, 2002; Denton, 2002; McLaughlin and Pitcock, 2009). High-quality instruction may also be enhanced by enacting hiring practices that give preference to effective and motivated teachers and by providing teachers with support during the summer program through coaching (McCombs, Kirby, and Mariano, 2009).

Aligned School-Year and Summer Curricula

Aligning the school-year and summer curricula also may improve the effectiveness of summer programming (Boss and Railsback, 2002; McLaughlin and Pitcock, 2009; Beckett, 2008). This content alignment can take two forms. First, the content of summer programs might be aligned with that of the prior grade to provide remediation on core concepts that students have failed to master. Second, the content could align to the upcoming school year so that students have previewed core concepts and have a head start toward mastery.

Engaging and Rigorous Programming

Many of the experts also recommend expanding the curriculum beyond remediation (Bell and Carrillo, 2007; Boss and Railsback, 2002; McLaughlin and Pitcock, 2009; Beckett, 2008). This recommendation is intended to promote comprehensive programs that go beyond "drill-and-kill" instruction and provide students with (1) expanded learning through innovative instruction that accelerates learning and (2) opportunities for enrichment. There are two reasons for this recommendation. First, for students to benefit from additional instruction, they must attend. Providing students with interesting, engaging enrichment opportunities is considered a method of promoting attendance in voluntary programs. Second, some experts also want the instructional methods and experiences of summer to feel different for students and to propel students forward in their learning.

Maximized Participation and Attendance

Because we know that students need to attend these programs to benefit from them (Borman, Benson, and Overman, 2005; Borman and Dowling, 2006; McCombs, Kirby, and Mariano, 2009), recruiting students into the programs and then maintaining their attendance are critical. Options for recruiting include mandating the program and incentivizing participation. Incentives could include payments, prizes, parental pledges, parental benefits, bus passes, and enrichment opportunities. The main question here is whether to mandate participation; however, mandating attendance is improbable without the threat of retention in grade, which would apply to only a very small percentage of students who would benefit from summer programming.

Sufficient Duration

Research shows a link between dosage and achievement outcomes; however, it does not clearly specify the appropriate duration for summer programs. McLaughlin and Pitcock (2009) recommend that programs be a minimum of 80 hours in total, while Winship et al. (2005) recommend that programs be constructed with a much higher number of hours (360)—nine hours a day, five days a week, for eight weeks.

Involved Parents

Cooper, Charlton, et al. (2000) found that programs that included a parental involvement component were associated with more positive achievement effects than those that did not. There are a number of reasons that involving parents might be an effective component of a summer program. First, gaining parental buy-in for a program should increase enrollment and attendance. Second, outreach to parents can include information about methods of expanding learning opportunities in the home, which could increase at-home learning as well.

Evaluations of Effectiveness

Program quality can be strengthened through evaluation (Bell and Carrillo, 2007; Boss and Railsback, 2002; Denton, 2002; McLaughlin and Pitcock, 2009; Beckett, 2008). By evaluating what works well and what does not, providers can make adjustments that improve program quality in later years. In addition, establishing an evaluation can help clarify program objectives, levers of change, and needed supports.

Overall, the programs with evaluations that we studied tended to align their summer programming with many of the recommendations presented here. For instance, the programs examined in the rigorous studies provided reading and/or mathematics instruction, used a curriculum that aligned with the school-day curriculum, had small class sizes (typically 15 or fewer students), provided professional development opportunities to teachers in an effort to improve quality and consistency, and included an evaluation component.

In addition to these recommendations, the National Summer Learning Association posts quality recommendations for program infrastructure and delivery of programming (Table 3.1) for summer learning programs that provide a comprehensive, enriching learning experience for students and provide a "unique summer culture" that differs from the school year.

While many of these recommendations align with those recommended by others (e.g., individualizing instruction, evaluating program effectiveness, providing staff with professional development, developing external partnerships), they also move beyond them by calling for long-term funding plans, a clear vision, development of a summer culture, and recruitment of culturally competent staff.

Table 3.1
National Summer Learning Association Quality Standards

Category	Recommendations
Program infrastructure	
Purpose	Program has mission and vision statements that are grounded in the needs of its community. Program sets annual goals for youth and for the organization that drive a continuous cycle of data collection, evaluation, and quality improvement. Program has evidence that it is meeting its goals and the needs of stakeholders.
Finance and sustainability	Program develops and implements a clear strategic plan and aligned fundraising plan. Program shares information about the program with key stakeholders to promote sustainability.
Planning	Program is designed to allocate enough time, staff, and resources to promote positive academic and developmental youth outcomes. Program has a proactive summer program planning process that is inclusive of all key stakeholders and connected to the goals of the program. Program has a comprehensive structure in place for all programming throughout the summer, in advance of the session.
Staff	Program's recruitment and staffing process intentionally yields culturally competent staff with relevant skills. Program staff is empowered to manage the program and has a voice in organizational decisions. Program provides extensive opportunities for staff development and advancement before, during, and after the session.
Partnerships	Program builds and maintains strong linkages with partners, including community organizations, the public school system, and government agencies, that are supportive of its mission and have a vested interest in the program's success. Program has a formal structure for communication and data sharing with all key external partners. Program builds and maintains strong linkages with families.
Point of service	
Individualized	Program assesses young people's needs early in the program and develops individualized strategies for meeting program goals.
Intentional	Activity planning and execution shows intentional focus on meeting learning goals and use of research-based instructional methods.
Integrated	Programming builds skills, knowledge, and behaviors that promote academic success and healthy development. Activities show a blend of academic strategies and social/emotional development strategies throughout the entire day.
Unique program culture	Program creates a "summer culture" that is different from the school year and promotes a sense of community.

SOURCE: National Summer Learning Association, undated(b).

Conclusions

Research shows that voluntary summer programs, mandatory summer programs, and at-home reading programs can all have positive effects on student achievement. It appears that increased productive learning time on academic tasks leads to achievement gains (or the mitigation of loss) for students.

However, summer learning programs do not guarantee positive achievement for enrollees. Students need to attend regularly, and programming needs to be high-quality and aligned with student needs. Research indicates that several factors may be related to improved program effectiveness, including provision of individualized instruction, parental involvement, and small class sizes. In addition, expert opinion generated from studies of summer school and regular school suggests that high-quality instruction (ensured through careful hiring and professional development), aligning academic content with school-year content, maximizing student participation and attendance, providing engaging learning experiences, and evaluating outcomes will all contribute to high-quality summer programming.

Summer learning programs can have short-term effects, but what is more compelling to decisionmakers is the effectiveness of programming over the long term. If gains fade by the next spring, summer programming may not be worth the investment relative to other interventions. A few studies have looked at whether effects carry over for two years and have found that positive effects persist (Jacob and Lefgren, 2004; McCombs, Kirby, and Mariano, 2009). However, no study has addressed whether those gains persist *after* two years. In addition, not enough research has examined the effectiveness of participating in multiple years of summer programming. Given that the effects of summer learning loss are cumulative, it is reasonable to hypothesize that summer learning gains due to programming might be cumulative as well. Indeed, one study of an at-home reading program confirms this hypothesis. However, the one study of a multiyear classroom-based summer program highlighted the problems of getting students to attend frequently enough to reap benefits. Thus, a key question that remains is whether one can construct a voluntary, classroom-based summer program that sustains high attendance levels to increase the possibility of cumulative effects.

The next two chapters address other obstacles that districts face in developing summer learning programs: cost (Chapter Four) and implementing, sustaining, and scaling high-quality programs (Chapter Five).

CHAPTER FOUR

Costs of Summer Programming

This chapter examines the costs of providing a particular kind of summer programming: programs that operate at scale (which we define as 1,000 or more students) with a focus on academics that are delivered primarily to disadvantaged children in grades K–8. The goal is to identify both the monetary and in-kind costs of this type of program, which we refer to in this chapter as a "summer learning program," to provide useful information to school districts that wish to develop these programs. To this end, we addressed four questions:

- What are the respective costs of externally led and school district–led summer learning programs that serve a large number of students?
- What are the sources of cost variation across these summer learning programs?
- Do school districts spend less on summer learning programs than on the academic school year on a per-pupil, per-week basis?
- What are the typical funding sources for summer learning programs?

To answer these questions, we first reviewed the literature on summer learning program costs, the findings from which are summarized here. Because these estimates did not capture the full costs of large-scale, academically oriented programs, we conducted our own data collection from seven providers to develop more comprehensive cost estimates. We also collected information on the sources of funds typically used to operate summer programs, which we also report in this chapter. We describe our costing methods in general terms here and provide a more detailed account in the appendix. To maintain source anonymity, discussions of cost and resource data do not identify the providers.

Evidence from the Literature

To our knowledge, there has been no comprehensive cost study of summer school–only programs. (Chapter One includes a description of the methods for our literature review.) The best approximation of such a study is The Wallace Foundation report

The Cost of Quality Out-of-School-Time Programs (Grossman et al., 2009), which separates summer costs from year-round OST programming. For our purposes, their cost estimates—approximately \$2–\$4 per slot per hour—are of limited value because they include all types of summer programs (both academically oriented and not), and the programs are a part of year-round OST offerings rather than summer-only programs, in which per-slot, per-hour costs are likely higher.[1]

To obtain estimates for large-scale, academically oriented programs offered during the summer only (and not year-round), we identified five reports on individual programs that included sufficient cost information to derive rough estimates. Table 4.1 summarizes estimates presented in those reports. From these figures, we estimate a cost range of \$7 to \$14 per slot per hour.[2] Even these costs likely underestimate the actual costs of summer programming, however. First, they do not examine full program *expenditures*, which would capture all monetary outlays for components of the program such as staffing, curricular development, materials, facilities, food, and transportation. Instead, the reports typically considered what it might cost to operate a summer program by examining only the total *revenues* allocated by one source of funds that was intended to cover most of the costs of the program. Since most programs draw on more than one source of funding (e.g., school district transportation and facilities budgets, the federally subsidized meal program, program funds set aside for the summer learning program), considering only one funding source can underestimate the full costs. Second, these estimates overlook the value of nonmonetary services or hidden costs, such as the value of donated goods and services provided by volunteers, which can reduce direct outlays for staffing, and, according to one study (Grossman et al., 2009) account for about 15 percent of a typical summer program's budget.

Finally, to take a summer or OST program to scale usually requires the addition of central office staff to coordinate or oversee the functions of the program's multiple sites. Looking across studies pertaining to either summer or OST programming, we found only one that distinguished the level at which costs were incurred. In a

[1] Note that we refer to the program cost per *slot* rather than per *enrollee*. Cost per *enrollee* is the total cost of the program divided by its total enrollment (Grossman et al., 2009). Cost per *slot* is the total cost of the program divided by average daily attendance (i.e., the typical number of students present on any given day). Especially in the case of summer school, expressing costs by slot better represents the true costs of a program per individual because it divides the cost of services by the typical number of recipients who consumed them. As described in the appendix, we believe that expressing costs in units of slots rather than enrollment is the most fair and reasonable way to present a range of summer learning program costs. This approach takes into account the elevated rates of absenteeism that summer learning programs often encounter relative to compulsory schooling during the academic year. However, since many school districts budget for summer programs based on projected total enrollment rather than total slots, we also discuss costs per enrollee in the appendix.

[2] The per-enrollee cost is lower than the per-slot cost of a given program, since total enrollments exceed average daily attendance (slots). Grossman et al. (2009) reported that per-enrollee costs were 75 percent of per-slot costs for the summer portion of year-round OST programs. We assumed the same relationship between enrollee and slot costs for the five academically oriented summer programs.

Table 4.1
Estimates per Enrollee from Existing Studies of Summer Programming Costs

				Services Included in the Estimate					
Location	Study	Cost per Enrollee per Hour (2010 $)	Curricular Focus	Instructional Staff	Central Office Staff	Materials	Transportation	Maintenance and Operations	Details
Pennsylvania	Conley and Rooney (2007)	5.54	Remediation	√	X	√	X	√	Modeled on inputs for Portland summer school remediation program
South Carolina	Monrad and May (2001)	5.70	Remediation	√	X	?	√	?	Survey of 79 out of 86 school districts; 74 offered summer programs that ranged from 10 to 31 days and 3 to 7 hours per day
BELL	Chaplin and Capizzano (2006)	9.26	Math, literacy, and enrichment	√	√	√	X	X	No cost detail; $1,500 per-student estimate As of 2005, BELL operated at a smaller scale for 8 hours per day and used a uniform math and literacy curriculum across its 5 locations
Austin, TX	Curry (2001)	9.95	Balanced literacy	√	√	√	√	X	The program operated in 12 elementary schools for 19 days and 4 hours per day
New Mexico	Goetze and Price (2009)	10.19	Extended learning time in high-poverty schools	√	√	√	?	?	K–3 Plus; participating schools usually offered 25 extra school days at the end of or prior to the traditional school year

NOTE: √ = Service included in cost estimate. X = Service not included in cost estimate. ? = Could not be determined from the data provided.

study of a year-round after-school literacy-based program that served approximately 5,000 elementary-age children annually in five California cities, Arbreton et al. (2008) estimated that 44 percent of total expenses were incurred at the city level. Of these expenditures, 71 percent were directed to salaries for positions such as literacy directors, operations directors, and executive directors. Facilities costs accounted for 9 percent of city-level expenditures. This example indicates that central office–level expenses can command a significant share of an overall summer learning program budget. Note that the three highest cost estimates of the five summer-only program studies listed in Table 4.1 at least partially included the cost of central planning and oversight, whereas the two lowest cost estimates did not.

Cost Estimates for Select Summer Learning Programs

To capture the full costs of academically oriented summer learning programs and to analyze the factors that most influenced their costs, we conducted our own data collection from seven selected programs: six classroom-based summer learning programs and one books-only summer program. We selected these programs in one of two ways. In some cases, we obtained a high-quality research report that identified positive effects of the particular summer program on students' academic outcomes. In other cases, we interviewed summer learning experts who recommended the programs as meeting four conditions: they are currently operational, they serve at least 1,000 children at any level between kindergarten and eighth grade, they are reputed to provide high-quality programming or they have high-quality evaluations of student outcomes that indicate success, and they are centrally run to provide a relatively uniform experience across multiple school sites. We identified a total of seven classroom-based summer programs that met these criteria, and six agreed to share cost data with us. We included the books-only program based on recent research about its effects (James Kim, 2006; Kim and White, 2008) to examine the costs of a summer learning program that is not classroom-based. These seven programs by no means generalize to all summer learning provider types in the United States, but based on interviews with experts, we have some confidence that the programs included here are representative of a relatively small group of high-quality programs that serve a large number of students. To maintain anonymity, we refer to these programs as Providers A through G.

Through semistructured phone interviews with the directors or financial officers of these programs, we sought to collect the complete set of actual expenditures and in-kind services associated with the provision of the program, including central office administrative functions, such as quality assurance and fundraising, and site-level functions, such as instruction, student transportation, and meal provision. Four primary factors determine a program's cost:

- *Enrollment.* The number of children, their age distribution, the percentage who actually attend, and their level of needs all affect cost.
- *Quantity.* Quantity refers to the number of hours per day, days per week, and weeks per year that a program operates. Often, programs that operate for a greater combined total number of hours can distribute the fixed costs of operating a program across a greater number of hours, thus reducing the hourly cost per enrollee.
- *Quality.* The quality of the program, as measured by structural elements such as student-to-instructor ratios, minimum education and training required of instructors, and the quality of the physical environment, as well as by process measures such as classroom management techniques, use of class time, and teacher-child interactions, also affects the cost.
- *Prices of resources.* Prices of resources can differ substantially, depending on the regional costs of goods and services, the characteristics of the local teacher labor market (where a more senior demographic can drive up costs), and accessibility to the program (where the availability of public transit systems, for example, can obviate the need for the provision of pupil transportation).

To standardize our estimates across programs that, in practice, operate for a different number of hours per day and weeks per year, we constructed per-slot, per-summer estimates in two steps. First, we multiplied the actual per-hour, per-slot administrative, instructional, and curriculum costs for each program (which are based only on those cost categories for which data were uniformly available)[3] by a uniform number of six hours per day and five weeks per summer. To each program's cost, we then added imputed values for transportation, school facilities, and food.[4] Although each program does not in actuality provide the same level of school facilities, food, and transportation to its students, we applied these costs as if they did to (1) account for these costs in cases in which the information was missing and (2) hold constant those elements of a summer programming that do not relate to instructional staff, curriculum, or administration. These latter three cost categories are of the utmost interest, as discussed next.

Figure 4.1 presents our best estimates of what it would cost for school districts and external providers to offer a summer learning program to a large number of students for six hours a day over five weeks in the summer. They range from $7 to $19 per slot per hour, which includes costs for classroom-based programming and uniform, imputed values for the cost of food, transportation, and facilities. (We applied these

---

3 These cost categories include central office administration and site-level costs for staff wages and benefits, instructional and administrative materials, staff development, and contracted services. See Table A.1 in the appendix for details and costs for each category.

4 These imputed per-slot, per-summer costs were $181 for facilities, $59 for transportation, and $105 for food. We did not apply costs for facilities, food, or transportation to the books-only program because it does not require any of these expenditures during the summer. Costs for food at this program's three family literacy nights are included, however.

Figure 4.1
Cost Estimates for Selected Summer Learning Programs, per Slot per Summer, 2009

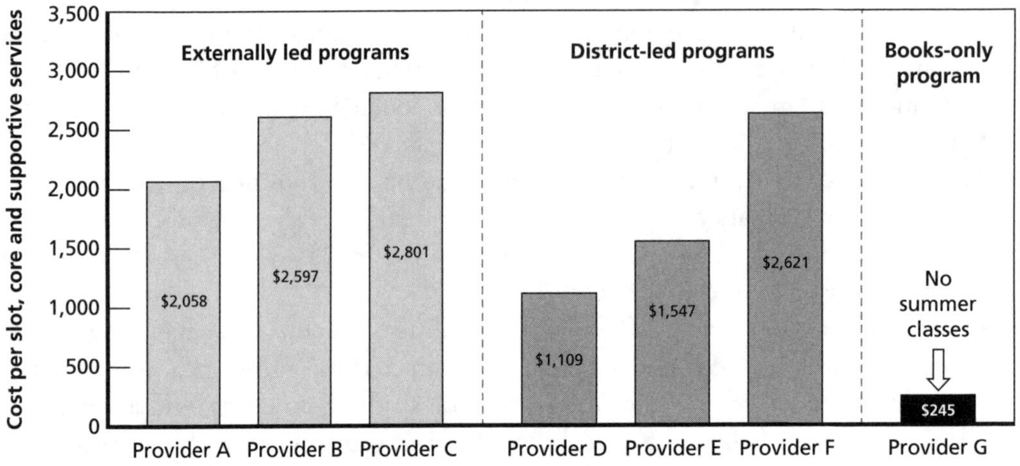

NOTE: The hourly rate for core services was applied to a hypothetical 25-day summer schedule of six hours per day. The total also includes uniform, imputed values for food, transportation, and facilities. Costs adjusted to U.S. national average to account for regional differences in the price of labor.
RAND *MG1120-4.1*

imputed values to each program because only a subset of programs tracked these costs. The costs for transportation, food, and facilities are considered later in this chapter.) This corresponds to $1,109–$2,801 per slot per summer.

As the figure shows, programs led by external providers (Providers A, B, and C) are generally more expensive than those led by districts (Providers D, E, and F). (We explain the reasons behind these differences in the next section.) Providers A, B, and C are national nonprofit organizations that operate in multiple cities in the United States and serve at least 1,000 students apiece. Each operates a school-based model that provides academic instruction and enrichment activities. Provider A directly operates its program by partnering with public school districts to operate summer learning programs that primarily target disadvantaged youth. In contrast, Providers B and C have affiliates that are usually led by private schools or, sometimes, nonprofit organizations. These, too, target disadvantaged students, though Provider C also targets high-achieving youth.

The district-led providers (Providers D, E, and F) each operate a summer program within their given district in some but not all school campuses. They, too, offer academic instruction and enrichment activities during the day. None is strictly remedial, but the programs tend to target disadvantaged or underperforming youth.

The seventh program (Provider G) is the books-at-home program and the only one included here that does not deliver academic content in classrooms led by adults. In this program, elementary-aged students receive three teacher-taught lessons during the spring of the regular school year and then are mailed ten books during the summer.

Each book is matched to the child's interest and reading skill level. Aside from the books themselves, the cost of the program includes three family literacy events held during the summer, as well as program administration, including mailing, data collection, and pre- and post-testing of children in the program.[5] Although Provider G served fewer than 1,000 students, we include it to offer a cost contrast to the classroom-based models of the other six.

Not surprisingly, the summer books-only program was far less expensive, costing $245 per slot per summer. As described in Chapter Two, books-only programs have been shown to improve reading scores; however, classroom-based programs may result in additional positive outcomes that the books-only programs cannot effect, such as mathematics achievement and improvements in safety, nutrition, behavioral or social outcomes, or recreational opportunities during the summer.

In light of the small number of providers in this sample and the lack of data about certain in-kind resources, the data reported should be interpreted as suggestive, lower-bound estimates of the funding levels required for the provision of summer learning programs. Despite its limitations, this cost analysis provides new insight into the structure and costs of summer learning programs that serve large numbers of students. They offer information about a hypothetical scenario in which each program operates for the same duration and offers the same level of transportation, food, and facilities to isolate the factors related to the administration of the summer learning programs (i.e., core services).

Sources of Cost Variation Across Programs

To understand the sources of the variation in overall estimated costs shown in Figure 4.1, we turn to a more detailed breakdown of the costs for summer learning programs. We present these costs in terms of two broad categories: core services and supportive services. In core services, we include central office costs, the cost of site-based instruction, administrative costs, and the costs of materials, such as books, and supplies. In supplemental services, we include food, facilities, and transportation, the costs of which were more difficult to track.

Core Services: Central Office and Site-Based Instructional and Administrative Costs

In this section, we focus on the costs of operating the central office and the site-level costs associated with instruction and administration. Note that because the books-only program did not have this structure, we exclude it from this discussion. However, the detailed costs for the program are reported in the appendix.

---

[5] Note that the books-only program cost estimates exclude the three lessons offered by teachers during the academic year.

Although we collected cost data from six classroom-based providers, they in fact operate what are eight distinct programs. Provider C is a national program with affiliates that either are hosted by private schools or are themselves nonprofit organizations. The nonhosted affiliates that are nonprofit organizations bear a greater proportion of the total economic costs of the program than do the affiliates hosted at private schools, which subsidize the costs of administration, facilities, and food. To isolate the unsubsidized costs of the program, in the appendix, we separately report average costs for hosted sites (i.e., affiliates operated by and at private school campuses) and the average costs for nonhosted sites (i.e., where nonprofit organizations run the summer program). In this section, however, we list only the hosted sites for Provider C, since its core summer school services do not differ between hosted and nonhosted sites.

We break Provider D into two parts in Table 4.2 to reflect the distinct programmatic differences between its morning academic program (funded by one source) and its afternoon program, which serves only a portion of the morning students (and is funded by another source). Whereas the morning session consists of instruction in math and English language arts by certified public school teachers, the afternoon consists of art and recreational sessions led by community-based artists. For Provider D, however, we add these costs together to provide per-summer per-slot and per-hour per-slot estimates, as shown in Figures 4.1 and 4.2, respectively.

Figure 4.2 shows costs for core services ranging from $5 to $16 per slot per hour for the summer learning programs. As described earlier, the amounts uniformly exclude the cost of food, transportation, and facilities, even for programs that track expenditures on those items. This was done for two reasons: Only a subset of programs tracked these costs, and school districts routinely provide these services from funds outside summer learning program budgets. (The costs of transportation, food, and facilities are considered in a subsequent section.)

There are three primary reasons that externally led summer learning programs have more expensive core services: differences in class size, central office functions, and nonstaff costs, such as books and supplies. First, the single largest effect on cost is the student-to-instructor ratio, even after adjusting for variance in the programs' minimum requirements for their instructors. The externally led programs have lower ratios, as shown in Table 4.2.[6] The least expensive program, on an hourly basis (Provider D), had by far the largest student-to-instructor ratio (18.4 students per teacher),

---

[6] Although the student-to-teacher ratio was the program element most highly correlated with cost, differences in minimum teacher qualifications had the second strongest effect on costs. Although the public school districts hired certified teachers for at least the morning (academic) portion of the summer program, they typically hired fewer instructors per student than the other programs. Thus, the extra cost associated with hiring certified teachers was offset by the savings realized from the increased student-to-teacher ratio (see the appendix for detailed costs per classroom teacher per hour). For example, Providers D and E placed a certified teacher as a lead instructor in each classroom but did not pair them with aides in every classroom. Almost all other programs, by contrast, blended their instructional staff by pairing certified or lead/mentor teachers (usually a year-round teacher in either public or private school) with assistant teachers enrolled in high school or college.

Table 4.2
Programmatic Structure of Selected Summer Learning Programs

	Externally Led Programs			District-Led Programs				Books-Only Program
Characteristic	**Provider A**	**Provider B**	**Provider C (hosted sites)**	**Provider D (academic portion)**	**Provider D (recreational portion)**	**Provider E**	**Provider F**	**Provider G**
Grade levels served	K–8	K–8	Middle	K–5	K–5	K–8	Middle	4th grade
Year of cost data collection	2009	2009	2009	2009	2009	2009	2010	2007
Total number of slots (average number of students per day)	2,661	1,571	2,211	6,510	794	4,800	1,300	370
Hours per day	6.5	6	5	4	4	6	6.5	NA
Weeks per summer	5	5	5	5	5	4	5	NA
Number of students per adult in classroom	7.8	4.6	3.4	18.4	20	8.7	3.8	NA
Professional teacher in each classroom			X	√ (morning only)	X	√ (morning only)	√ (morning only)	NA
Public schools are primary host		X	X					
Target disadvantaged students								
Target high-achieving students	X	X		X	X	X	X	X
Serve special education students	X	X	X			X		

SOURCE: Phone interviews and data from program providers.

NOTE: √ = yes. X = no. NA = not applicable.

Figure 4.2
Cost Estimates for Core Summer Services, per Slot per Hour, 2009

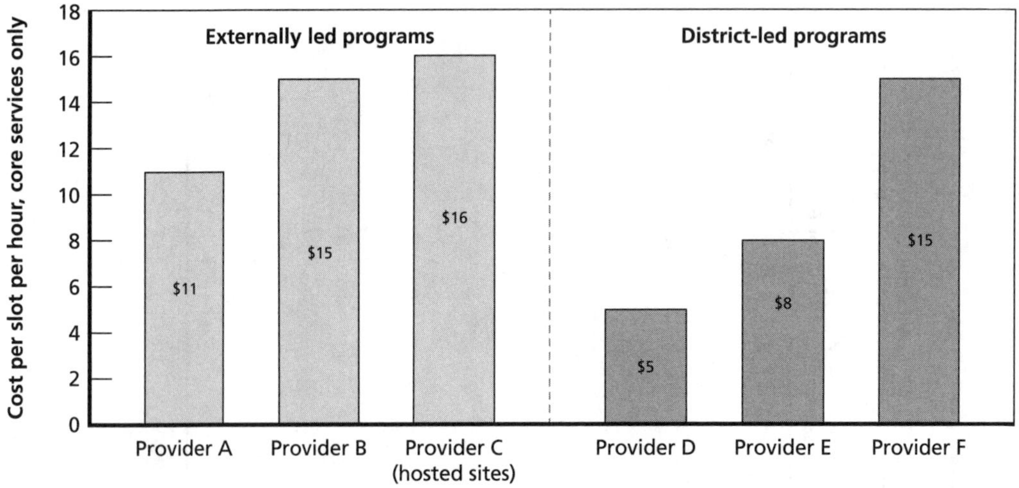

NOTE: All estimates shown exclude the cost of supportive services (food, transportation, facilities). Costs adjusted to U.S. national average to account for regional differences in the price of labor.
RAND *MG1120-4.2*

and it also served the greatest number of students (which can help achieve economies of scale). In contrast, the most expensive program had 3.4 students per instructor. The most expensive program within a school district is the one that most closely approximated the student-to-instructor ratio of externally led programs (Provider F, with 3.8 students per classroom-based adult). Externally led providers typically spent almost $3 more per slot per hour on school instructors and school administrators than did public school district programs.

Second, externally led programs incurred greater costs to run their central offices. They spent an average of $1.80 more per slot per hour on central office functions than did school districts. The most obvious reason is that the central office in an externally led organization performed more functions than a district's summer school central office. As national nonprofit organizations, the externally led providers had staff who raised funds for the organization or affiliates; traveled to oversee the quality of the provision of services at providers' sites; recruited sites, teachers, and students; and developed curricula. These providers also expended funds on operating costs, such as leasing and maintaining the central office space, information technology, accounting, and tax services, costs that school districts often absorbed in budgets separate from summer school.

District-led providers, on the other hand, did not perform all of these functions. They tended to employ fewer district staff to operate their summer learning programs. Only Provider F employed multiple full-time-equivalent (FTE) staff members to work on summer programming, and this was due, in part, to its first-year status and larger fixed costs to develop the curriculum, market the program, and recruit teachers. The districts we surveyed also typically encountered fewer fundraising requirements, although they did report pressure to raise private funds, as documented in the section "Financial Sources for Summer School Programming," later in this chapter. In addition, they incurred minimal or no within-district travel costs to oversee sites. They recruited from a preexisting pool of public school teachers (many of whom already work in the school during the rest of the year), used school district office space at no programmatic cost, and typically incurred lower student recruitment costs.

Finally, in addition to central office costs, externally led providers expended slightly more on average than districts on the nonstaff costs incurred at the school level (operating costs such as books, supplies, field trips, and information technology). Providers A, B, and C expended almost $1 more per slot per hour on school-based nonstaff costs compared to districts that had been operating their programs for multiple years (i.e., Providers D and E). While externally led providers may incur greater expenses than the two school districts for increased field trips (for example), it is also probable that district-led providers obtained a greater proportion of their funds for back-office functions from sources external to the summer school budget relative to externally led providers.

Supportive Services: Meals, Facilities, and Transportation

In addition to the cost of core services, each of the six classroom-based programs also incurred expenses for meals, facilities, and transportation. Yet funds for these expenses, particularly meals and facilities, often came from sources outside summer school program budgets and thus they were not uniformly tracked. For example, Provider A's sites typically paid for only a portion of the cost of facilities ($0.70 per slot per hour, on average) because Provider A required school districts to provide this access in kind. Likewise, Provider A's sites did not pay for food. Instead, funds for meals came from districts' school nutrition programs, which partially or fully subsidized the cost of meals for students in public schools during summer months. Finally, some programs did not offer transportation at all, whereas others offered it at a level that matched bus service provided during the school year.

The patchwork of subsidies for and monetary expenditures on facilities, food, and transportation rendered direct comparisons of each service across each program impossible. However, in a few cases, programs did pay for the full costs associated with the respective services, providing some insight into the potential per-hour and per-summer costs of each.[7]

By virtue of an organizational difference among its affiliates, Provider C, in particular, sheds light on costs that are often hidden. A minority of Provider C's affili-

[7] Note that all figures discussed here are included in the detailed cost data set in the appendix and have been adjusted to reflect the national average cost in 2009 dollars.

ates were themselves nonprofit organizations leasing space at school sites, while the majority of affiliates were run by and at private schools. Private school affiliates offered a wide range of in-kind goods and services that the nonprofit affiliates typically did not receive, such as office space and related amenities, photocopying and scanning capabilities, utilities, equipment (such as computers and software), telecommunication and Internet access, website maintenance, insurance, bookkeeping, accounting and tax services, maintenance and janitorial services, postage, certain classroom supplies, and full use of classroom and athletic facilities at the host campus. The net difference of $349 per student per summer between nonhosted and hosted sites indicates the combined value of such services.

Disaggregating some of these costs, nonhosted Provider C affiliates spent additional increments (on a per-slot, per-summer basis) on the following services: $28 for administrative services, $20 for student recruitment, $63 for contracted services like accounting, and $181 for facilities. Since all other programs used classroom space at a subsidized rate or even gratis, $181 per slot per summer (or $1.21 per slot per hour) is the only approximation we found of the full costs associated with the use of school buildings among the seven selected programs we studied.[8]

There are, however, more data on transportation. All three public school districts we studied offered transportation for children enrolled in their summer programs, whereas only some externally led school sites did so. In the districts, these costs were $0.29 per slot per hour for Provider D, $0.50 per slot per hour for Provider E, and $2.08 per slot per hour for Provider F (or $46, $60, and $338 per slot per summer, respectively). Since Provider F's program was in its first year, it is likely that Providers D and E offered more seasoned estimates. Nevertheless, a large variation in transportation costs remains and is due, in part, to differences in distance traveled. The large variance indicates the importance of incorporating local factors into transportation estimates. For the purposes of imputing costs for transportation to develop per-summer cost estimates, we used the average per-slot, per-hour cost of transportation from Providers D and E only.[9]

The minimum cost expended on meals was the per-pupil, per-meal rate for the federally subsidized breakfast and lunch programs in public school districts. But some providers (Provider F, in particular) sought to provide higher-quality meals as a marketing tool and to increase the nutritional value of the food. The per-slot, per-hour cost

---

8 As an interesting point of contrast, the San Francisco Unified School District leases school facilities to third parties during summer months. It publishes a tiered rate schedule by the day or week and by the number of classrooms. For example, a weekly rate for the use of 10–15 classrooms was $1,165 in summer 2010. Assuming that a summer school day that is five hours long and serves an average of six children per classroom, each day nets to a facilities cost of $0.78 per slot per hour. The 2010 rate schedule is no longer available online; for the 2011 rate schedule, see San Francisco Unified School District (2011).

9 As noted elsewhere, these costs were first adjusted to 2009 dollars and averaged nationally across each provider's programs.

of meals ranged from a low of $0.47 (Provider E) to a high of $2.14 (Provider F). This equates to a range of $54 to $348 per slot.

How Summer Costs Compare to School-Year Costs

Given the constraints on resources, it would be ideal to compare the long-term benefits and costs of summer school to those of other educational interventions to test their relative merits. Yet education, as compared to other sectors such as health, has a relatively small set of studies that compare the costs and effectiveness of respective interventions (Ross, Barkaoui, and Scott, 2007). Because the long-term effects of summer learning programs are unknown, we instead sought to contextualize the total cost estimates presented here by comparing them to weekly per-slot costs during the school year.

We found that summer programming offered by a district tends to be less expensive on a per-week, per-pupil basis than education costs during the academic year:

- Provider D's summer program cost $221 per slot per week, compared to the $400 per slot per week spent during the school year (56 percent).
- Provider E's summer program cost $309 per slot per week in the summer compared to the $490 per slot per week spent during the academic year (63 percent).
- By contrast, Provider F's summer program cost *more* per week than expenditures during the regular school year. Provider F's summer program cost $524 per slot per week in the summer compared to the $431 per slot per week spent during the academic year (121 percent). However, Provider F's costs were outliers, which may be due, in part, to start-up costs associated with its first year of operation.

There are several reasons that the costs of Provider D and Provider E's district-led summer learning program were significantly lower than the cost of their compulsory schooling. In our interviews, school district administrators attributed the lower costs primarily to the significantly reduced level of support services for special education students and English language learners. In addition, the district provided fewer support services to schools during the summer session (e.g., curricular planning, accountability, reporting). Finally, certified teachers worked for reduced wages relative to academic-year wages, and summer learning programs used lower-cost staff for enrichment activities provided for half the day.

Financial Sources for Summer School Programming

Because funding was identified as the greatest challenge facing school districts that wish to offer summer programming, we sought information from the literature and conducted interviews with administrators in five school districts to identify key funding sources. Because some but not all of the districts are included among those for which we report costs, we refer to the districts here as District 1 through District 5. Five school districts are large, and we selected them because they currently operate publicly funded elementary or middle school summer learning programs that summer learning experts identified as innovative or of high quality.

Although funding for individual programs can vary from year to year, summer programs tend to draw on a common set of public and private funding sources (Fairchild, Smink, and Stewart, 2009).

Federal Funding Sources

Among federal sources that often fund summer school, some are designed to support academic achievement while others are oriented toward child care, nutrition, and support to low-income families. These federal resources are generally allocated to states and communities through a variety of finance vehicles, including entitlement programs, which guarantee that all who are eligible are served by the program, and formula or block grants that provide states or communities with a fixed amount of funding. While our discussion focuses on the main federal sources of funding, they are only a few of the 103 funding sources that were identified by Dobbins-Harper and Bhat (2007) that could be used for youth program development initiatives.

More than 50,000 public schools across the country use Title I funding to provide additional learning opportunities for students at risk of failing to meet state and local academic standards (U.S. Department of Education, 2011). Title I grants are intended for schools with high percentages of children from low-income families, and they are provided to local education authorities (i.e., school districts), which then allocate funds to schools to help students who are at risk of not meeting the state academic standards. School districts that offer summer programming for disadvantaged students often devote a portion of their Title I allocation to fund it, as is described later. Note that, although Title I dollars can be used for a variety of programs, they are not explicitly targeted to summer programs; thus, summer programming competes with other potential uses of Title I funds in any given district. Furthermore, the allowable expenditures on Title I summer programs are the same as the allowable expenditures on Title I programs during the regular school year—namely, the use of licensed, Title I–certified teachers who supervise aides or paraprofessionals at a ratio of no more than two aides per certified teacher.

Another Elementary and Secondary Education Act–funded provision that can be used to provide summer learning opportunities is the 21st Century Community Learning Centers (21st CCLC) program. The 21st CCLC formula grants are awarded to state education agencies, which, in turn, competitively award the funds to school districts and applicant nonprofit organizations that have school-community partnerships. The goal of a 21st CCLC program is to provide academic enrichment opportunities for students who attend low-performing schools. The program is designed to operate during nonschool hours (although legislation has been proposed to increase the flexibility of the program to fund an increase in school hours).

Title I and 21st CCLC are two examples of frequent sources of federal funding for district-led summer programming. They can be combined, as is the case in District 1, which ran a program that served approximately 9,000 students in summer 2010. With a local nonprofit organization that provided arts programming, the district co-led the program with a combined budget of approximately \$3.85 million.[10] These funds comprised almost \$1 million in 21st CCLC funds, \$1.5 million in Title I funds, \$1 million in district general operations funds, \$350,000 in Title III funds,[11] and approximately \$100,000 in private philanthropic funds. The 21st CCLC funds financed community artists who worked at the school. This model is similar to District 2, which used approximately \$3.5 million in Title I funds in summer 2010 to finance the morning portion of a summer program for approximately 6,500 students at 30 elementary schools. The 21st CCLC funds provided for an afternoon program at fewer than ten of the 30 schools, led by contracted staff through the locality's recreational department and a CBO that served approximately 900 of the 6,500 children with recreational and artist-led activities.

Additional sources of funds for summer programming pertain to child care. The U.S. Department of Health and Human Services funds Temporary Assistance for Needy Families (TANF) and the Child Care and Development Fund (CCDF), which are sources of funding for child care. Since seeking employment often requires child care, TANF funds can cover the cost of such care for needy families with children. Most commonly, TANF dollars are used to supplement CCDF programs to support summer child care (see Relave and Flynn-Khan, 2007). CCDF resources, in turn, are used to subsidize the cost of child care for children under age 13 and are awarded to states according to per capita income, the number of children who are below age 5, and the ratio of children who benefit from the National School Lunch Program. The child-care services are provided to eligible families through certificates or contracts with practitioners that enable parents to select any legally operating child care provider. CCDF dollars currently support a variety of OST programs that operate during summers and school holidays (Child Care Bureau, 2009). None of the school districts in our sample relied on these funds for its summer program.

The U.S. Department of Housing and Urban Development authorizes Community Development Block Grants (CDBGs) to develop viable neighborhoods by providing decent housing, improved living environments, and expanded economic opportu-

10 Note that this figure does not include the cost of food (which was subsidized by the U.S. Department of Agriculture meals program), school facilities, or school district staff time, all of which were provided in kind to the summer program.

11 Title III is a federal program to provide funds for language instruction for English language learners and immigrant students.

nities for low- and moderate-income persons. CDBG funds are generally administered at the municipal level. While the majority of CDBG funds are typically directed to housing or infrastructure-related costs, they can also support OST programs, youth involvement, and community school initiatives (Fairchild, Smink, and Stewart, 2009).

Finally, another recent federal source of funding is the American Recovery and Reinvestment Act of 2009 (ARRA)—a subset of which has been set aside for School Improvement Grants—including a large amount of funding for education that could be used toward summer programming. More than $30 billion has been allocated to states and districts to support school reform and innovative programming through ARRA, and some of these funds were set aside to turn around low-performing schools through the School Improvement Grant. This funding was designed to be allocated through several existing funding streams, including Title I block grants, Title I Part A funding for local districts, the Race to the Top program (which is administered by governors and school districts), and the Innovation Fund (Fairchild, Smink, and Stewart, 2009). Unlike the programs described here, however, it is not anticipated that ARRA will be renewed, so it is not a long-term source of funding for summer programs.

This is a challenge facing District 3, which launched an ARRA-financed summer learning program for approximately 2,000 children in summer 2010. The program is funded primarily by a $10 million ARRA (Title I) allocation, divided between two years of summer programming. Given Title I restrictions, all ARRA-financed morning and afternoon activities are tied to academic activities, even though the afternoon programming is more recreational in nature and provided by contracted CBOs. To fund engaging but nonacademic programs (e.g., fencing) that were in high demand by students, the district also raised approximately $325,000 in grants from local foundations. While the program has generated considerable enthusiasm and enjoyed strong support from the district superintendent, the primary hurdle facing the program is to identify funds to sustain it beyond its two-year ARRA commitment.

State Funding Sources

Often, federal funds are used to complement existing state and locally sponsored summer youth programs. States have approved education initiatives and referendums, and municipalities have raised tax dollars in a variety of ways to fund youth programs (Sherman, Deich, and Langford, 2007). Some examples include special tax levies or the establishment of a nonprofit intermediary to pool funding sources (National League of Cities, 2009).

The Education Commission of the States found that 35 states and the District of Columbia have policies that either promote or mandate summer learning programs for academic remediation. Many states pay for those programs through their primary funding formula for public schools or through categorical funding (Griffith and Zinth, 2009). When provided through the primary funding formula, state funds are allocated to local school districts and schools based on a standard amount and then, depending on the state, allocated in equal or weighted amounts on a per-pupil basis. Categorical funds, on the other hand, are designed to reach particular populations of students (e.g., high-need, special education, or migrant students) or certain grade levels. However, as noted by Griffith and Zinth (2009), information on the exact amount of state funding for summer learning programs is not readily available.

In Districts 4 and 5, recurring funds from state initiatives have largely enabled the existence of summer programs. District 4's state legislature enacted a law allocating funds to school districts to provide additional supports to students at risk of not graduating from high school. District 4 received $12 million in 2010 under this law, half of which was dedicated to after-school programming. Ninety-five percent of the remaining $6 million went to the summer program, which served almost 5,000 children in summer 2010. In addition, a small portion of funds (totaling less than 5 percent of the summer school budget) came from local referendum dollars, a state program to fund desegregation, and a small amount of philanthropic donations (totaling less than $200,000). With the funds from the state graduation incentive law, District 4's summer school administrator has plans to expand the program in future years, although she acknowledges the considerable funding challenge were the summer program required to compete with other school district needs for scarce Title I and general operations funds.

Similarly, District 5's state legislature enacted legislation directing funds over a period of six years to low-performing, high-poverty schools to fund not only interventions but also preventative programs in early grades. District 5 has chosen to apply these funds to extend school time, including a summer program. State statutory measures to allocate funds to close achievement gaps have provided the foundation for districts in the state to choose interventions, and many have chosen summer programming. Collectively, state operational funds and a state program directed at early grades provide 85 percent of the $4.9 million that District 5 uses to finance its summer learning program.

Private Funding Sources

Private sources, such as philanthropic grants and parental fees, also fund summer programs. However, the share of private dollars that typically funds summer learning programs is unknown. There is more evidence regarding use of private funds for OST programs operated during the summer that are not necessarily focused on academics. In a survey of 111 non-district-provided "high-quality," year-round OST programs across six major cities, about 40 percent of the program budgets came from private funds, 33 percent from public funds, 20 percent from in-kind contributions, and the balance from parent fees (Grossman et al., 2009). For teen programs, parental fees (up to 2 percent of the budget) were avoided and instead offset with increased private funds (Grossman et al., 2009). A separate study found that parental fees accounted for the largest share (80 percent) of summer program revenues, with the remainder from federal, state, and local governments and from philanthropies (Weiss et al., 2009).

We are not aware of any summer learning program run by a school district that is funded solely through private sources—whether through philanthropic dollars or parent fees. In the cases in our sample, district-led programs did not assess parental fees, and the philanthropic funds obtained by the district covered only a small portion of their total budget (well below 10 percent). However, each district noted the desirability of philanthropic funds because those funds have the fewest restrictions, compared to federal, state, or local public sources.

Putting It All Together: Achieving Stable Funding Streams

The financial landscape for summer learning programs is stretched across a variety of sources, which places the burden of coordinating the many different requirements and provisions for those dollars on providers and summer learning advocates (Fairchild, Smink, and Stewart, 2009). Private providers who lack direct access to state or federal sources confront a more challenging fundraising task. However, a large number of school districts have been forced to make cuts to summer funds in the midst of a recession, placing some of the largest summer learning programs at risk.

In our interviews, administrators from the five school districts that run summer learning programs each independently confirmed the importance of connectedness to local politicians and community organizations. When asked which political or financial resources they deemed necessary for other school districts that wish to offer summer school programming, each stressed the importance of "community connections," which meant local capacity on the part of CBOs to offer activities that could be included in the summer school programming, as well as support from the superintendent, local politicians, and local foundations. Administrators from two of the five districts emphasized the importance of research that documents the positive impact of summer school on students' test scores as a means of obtaining sustained funding for summer school.

Each of the districts operated within constrained funding that caused them to make choices to cut programming or costs in either the summer of 2010 or future years as a means of sustaining the program. Three of the five districts realized costs savings through a reduction in the number of school campuses participating in the summer program. Reducing the number of campuses allowed districts to cut overhead costs, as fewer buildings needed an administrator and support staff, and it often reduced the number of bus transportation routes. However, the trade-off in reduced campuses was an increase in the number of enrollees per campus to numbers that were higher than they would have liked. In District 1, some of the campus buildings had more than 400 enrollees in the summer program.

While funding is undoubtedly the largest challenge facing school districts that wish to offer summer programming, district administrators also mentioned using the unique nature of summer learning programs as a marketing tool to raise funds. Administrators from three of the five districts stressed the independence of the summer learning program from the regular school year, even calling the summer learning program a "school district within a school district." In other words, summer learning providers could advertise to funders that they offer a more diverse, more fun, and more activity-based program. To underscore the distinction between summer and the academic year, one district operated its program in the middle of the summer to prevent overlap of the school-based summer and regular-year administrative staff, who are present in the building through June.

Nevertheless, absent consistent funding streams, such as dedicated tax levies, fundraising is a challenge for even summer providers with a long and successful track record. Programming for a large proportion of students often requires negotiation of local politics to secure and retain limited public financial support.

Conclusions

In this chapter, we provided a detailed account of the costs—and cost drivers—of selected summer learning programs that we hope will help districts and external providers decide whether to launch these programs and how to fund them. We conclude that providing a summer learning program can cost between $1,109 and $2,801 per student per summer for a five-week schedule that includes food, transportation, and facilities. We emphasized a number of points about these costs:

- They are lower for districts than they are for external providers.
- They are lower for summer programming than for education during the school year.
- The key cost driver is staffing, so lower student-to-instructor ratios have significant cost implications.
- Districts draw on multiple sources of funding at the federal and state levels and also cultivate community support from nonprofit organizations, local foundations, and city agencies.

The costs of summer programs are, of course, above and beyond what districts are required by their states to spend on educating students. District officials must therefore decide whether they find these programs cost-effective compared to other interventions. The research summarized in Chapters Two and Three can inform the value side of this calculation and identify the practices associated with strong outcomes. If district officials decide to support summer learning programs, they will also need to make trade-offs between quality and cost. We hope this cost analysis helps outline the parameters for those decisions. In the absence of data about the long-term effects of summer learning programs, we found no rigorous evidence on the cost-effectiveness of summer learning programs when compared to other potential interventions.

There are a number of funding sources available to support summer programming. However, for most funding streams, summer programs compete with other programs that use those funds. When funds have traditionally been used to support other programs, it is difficult for leaders to reallocate funding away from existing programs.

Districts and external providers have been able to combine multiple sources of support to sustain summer learning programs over time and to launch new programs despite the budget crises in so many states and school districts.

In the next chapter, we offer other information that we hope will help districts, external providers, funders, and policymakers decide whether to support summer learning programs: the actual experience of district officials and external providers in implementing these programs.

CHAPTER FIVE

Creating and Maintaining Summer Learning Programs: Lessons from the Field

This chapter draws on our field work to provide insights into district decisionmaking on summer learning programs. We synthesize interview data on why districts and others do, or do not, establish summer learning programs. For those that do provide programming, we summarize the barriers they faced in creating, sustaining, and scaling their programs and discuss how they overcame these barriers. We then refer back to the quality components presented in Chapter Three in considering how the programs we studied strove to ensure quality. This information should be useful to school district leaders and others considering or planning summer learning programs.

To gather this information, we conducted 66 interviews across 19 summer learning programs. Programs were operated by districts, cities, and other nondistrict providers, such as national nonprofit summer learning organizations. All the providers offered voluntary (and some offered mandatory) summer learning programs for youth in the summer of 2010.

Here, we present the results from the analysis of the data collected during our site visits and telephone interviews. We first report the reasons that districts and external providers offer summer learning programs and what we learned about their commitment to these programs. We then discuss the risks to and facilitators of programming in general. Although we make reference to funding and staffing as key facilitators, we refer readers to Chapter Four for a more detailed information of the costs of summer learning programs and the funding sources that districts are currently accessing. We then turn to the reported challenges and facilitators of ensuring quality. We end this chapter with a set of conclusions about district actions to launch, sustain, and scale summer learning programs.

Purposes and Commitments

Summer learning programs are offered to reduce summer learning loss and to prepare students to continue their education. However, reasons to offer a summer learning program vary within this overarching goal. For example, some programs aim to turn around low-performing schools. Others are targeted to eighth-grade and older students, with an expressed goal of reducing the high school dropout rate. Still other programs are offered only to middle school students, either to improve their achievement (e.g., in literacy or algebra) or to prepare them to make the transition to high school.

Program leaders described other, nonacademic, goals. For example, in Pittsburgh, leaders of the middle school summer learning program called the Summer Dreamers Academy talked about the importance of developing "soft skills" that their students need to be successful in high school and college. These skills include demonstrating appropriate behavior, maintaining a positive attitude, public speaking ability, good study habits, and the ability to work in teams. Interviewees in Minneapolis reported that their program addressed the "opportunity gap." They were striving to "give . . . students the same type of experience that students from middle-class families would have." A representative from the mayor's office in Baltimore reported that one of the city's goals was to keep students safe during the summer.

Although these nonacademic goals were espoused as important, many interviewees stressed that improved test scores were the most important goal of a school district's leadership. Interviewees in Pittsburgh, for example, lauded the superintendent for envisioning and supporting the program but added that he will not continue to support it if the data do not demonstrate that participating students' English language arts test scores have improved. Interviewees in Albuquerque worried that their students' progress would not be detected by the district benchmark tests and that the program would not be considered effective by the superintendent. Summer program staff there noted that students attending summer courses tended to be far below grade level—typically two or three years behind. Consequently, they were concerned that students' progress would not be apparent on the benchmark assessment results. They noted that there is no way that a summer program could help students who were two years behind catch up to their peers. One representative there asked, "Do we really want to make [summer programs] mandatory when we are short of money, given the uncertain payoff?" An interviewee from a national organization that partners with multiple school districts reported that she can demonstrate gains of three to five months over the summer and that the superintendent will still want to see the impact on state test scores. Other interviewees argued that as state test scores improve, summer programming becomes less important. A representative from Classroom, Inc., for example, observed that there were fewer summer opportunities throughout the district in New York City when test scores were improving.[1]

---

1 New York State recently changed its performance-level cut scores and many more students are now being identified at the lowest-performance level.

Overcoming Barriers to Launching and Maintaining Programs

Despite the ongoing concerns of some district leaders about the efficacy of summer learning programs, there are clearly districts and others committed to providing these programs. But even with high-level commitment and support, program leaders encountered challenges to launching, maintaining, and scaling their programs. We describe those challenges here, along with how they were overcome.

Early Challenges

We asked providers about the challenges they faced as they established their programs. Some interviewees described challenges in matching implementation strategies with expectations for summer learning programs. For example, the K–3 Plus summer learning program in Albuquerque was intended to accelerate learning for students in high-poverty schools so that they would start the school year ready to learn at grade level and not need remediation on material learned in the previous grade. The goal was to have students take summer classes from the same teacher they would be assigned to in the fall. Although this concept seems simple, implementing it proved extraordinarily complex. Teachers were not required to teach the summer program, so the teacher-student match did not always work. In addition, many teachers came to believe that they would have to cover material from the previous grade anyway, because not all students who would need remediation enrolled in the summer program. Therefore, teachers deviated from the curriculum and site leaders expressed frustration at what they saw as unattainable goals.

Another risk to building a summer learning program within a school district is the need for buy-in from other district staff members. Well-run district-based summer learning programs necessitate support from several district departments, including food services, facilities, transportation, libraries, information technology, and, in many cases, mathematics and language arts departments. Interviewees in the more mature sites reported that they had developed strong relationships with district departments over time. Sites with recent programs were struggling to navigate the district bureaucracy, particularly in the summer, when a lot of district staff take vacations. As described later, the ability to start planning for summer school the year before its launch was reported as a key facilitator in establishing necessary district support.

Interviewees from relatively new district-based summer learning programs also talked about the challenges involved in developing partnerships with local CBOs. Many of the district providers we interviewed were partnering with local CBOs to provide enrichment opportunities for their students. Most of the reported challenges were logistical and involved negotiating calls for proposals, contracts, and fee structures. Other, more indirect, CBO-related challenges focused on interpreting funding guidelines to determine, for example, whether Title I funding could cover programming provided by CBO staff. In some cases, certified teachers were asked to work hand-in-hand with CBOs to ensure that there were academic components of the enrichment programming.

Ongoing Challenges

Most of the ongoing challenges across the providers were related to funding. District administrators worried about what they considered to be the high costs of summer programming, based primarily on the costs of hiring certified teachers to teach small groups of students, given tight district budgets. As described in Chapter Four, districts often pull together funding from multiple sources to support summer learning programs. Some of this funding comes with strings attached, so program administrators, to secure the necessary funding, need to fully investigate what they can use it for and plan accordingly.

Other ongoing challenges to maintaining a summer learning program include lack of air conditioning and low or uncertain enrollment. As mundane as it might sound, the lack of air conditioning has been very problematic in some sites. In Baltimore, summer programs had to close for several days due to extreme heat in 2010 because many school facilities operating programs were not air-conditioned. Once they had closed for a few days, they found it difficult to attract students to come back to the program.

Barriers to Scale

Some providers reported challenges to expanding their programs. For example, Minneapolis summer learning leaders would like to expand the number of summer learning weeks (to eight) and the number of days of summer learning per week (to five). Their reported challenges go beyond funding and include teacher burnout, conflicts with days teachers are required to attend professional development prior to the regular school year, and conflicts with facilities work on the schools in the summer.

Even districts that have the capacity to scale do not necessarily have the interested students. None of the programs we examined were capturing more than half of their low-performing student populations. In Albuquerque, enrollment had grown but the program was still operating below capacity. In Baltimore, the programs were also operating below capacity. There were 6,000 middle school students eligible for the program and funding for 2,000 of them, but only 1,200 students enrolled.

Overcoming Barriers

Three of the barriers described here were fairly easy to overcome: developing relationships with district staff and with CBOs and ensuring access to facilities with air conditioning. Supportive leadership, hard work by qualified and dedicated staff, and program experience and maturation were key factors in building strong relationships with both district staff and CBOs. Experienced staff who have strong relationships with facilities departments can ensure access to buildings with air conditioning.

The program administrators we interviewed admitted that they work incredibly hard to support these programs. In Pittsburgh, the four year-round coordinators reported working 60 hours per week during the school year and 80 hours per week during the summer to start the program. Other providers reported similar levels of dedication and hard work. Coordinating a new program for large numbers of students necessitates advance planning and dedication by motivated and qualified staff members who can execute the program vision.

Supportive leadership was also described as important in launching programs and ensuring that they get the district operational funding they are allocated. Some interviewees stressed that the driver of the program needs to be the superintendent or, at minimum, a person who reports directly to the superintendent. Interviewees in Los Angeles, where several summer programs for elementary and middle school youth were cut, worried that leaders in the district were more interested in extending the school day than in supporting summer programs.

Unrealistic goals, insufficient funding, and low enrollment are more obstinate barriers. Setting realistic and implementable goals requires having a clear vision and the time to implement it. Interviewees stressed that they start planning for the next summer program on the day after the current summer program ends. Their planning is facilitated by a clear vision and objectives that they can share not only with their team but also with others throughout the district or city who will be involved in the planning. Interviewees in Pittsburgh noted that, because they had quickly established a clear vision to support both improved middle school literacy and "soft skills" through a camp-like program, they could do year-ahead marketing with students and teachers in the district.

Not all districts are able to dedicate qualified personnel to this planning. In Charlotte-Mecklenburg, interviewees reported that it takes six to nine months to plan a summer learning program and they did not have the staff to dedicate that time. According to multiple interviewees, parents and teachers both have made decisions about their summers by the end of February, necessitating early recruiting of these populations. Even districts in which staff can start planning for the next summer in the fall might have a hard time engaging district and board leadership, who are often unable to focus on the summer until the late spring, making it challenging to finalize budgets and contracts for summer personnel. And few districts are willing to commit to providing summer programming over multiple summers due to uncertainties in future funding.

A lack of funding was overcome in some sites through creativity. According to an interviewee from a national summer learning organization who has partnered with multiple school districts, "Success takes creativity in funding." As described in Chapter Four, providers sought and received funding from a myriad of federal (e.g., stimulus and 21st CCLC funding), state, and private funding streams. Less obvious sources of funding also supported these programs. In Dallas, AmeriCorps students were hired to provide instruction. In Denver, Summer Scholars hired teachers enrolled in administrative coursework who needed an unpaid administrative internship as site coordinators. As predicted in Chapter Four, interviewees also reported in-kind support from school districts, including the use of facilities and buses. Interviewees urged districts to find unspent Title I money and to press for local funding from unusual sources, such as police departments and other organizations concerned with youth safety during the summer. CBO interviewees in San Francisco and the Summer Scholars program in Denver further reported that their ability to provide data on program outcomes, including student and parent satisfaction, helped them obtain private funding. Another cost-saving strategy is to focus on the worst-performing schools or students to reduce the budget.

Not all sites were able to overcome a lack of funding. Charlotte-Mecklenburg cut its elementary student summer learning programs, despite finding that participating students were more likely to be promoted to the next grade if they had attended a summer learning program. They found that, in particular, the costs of transportation and running the air-conditioning systems in the schools were overwhelming. In Los Angeles, summer programs for both elementary and middle school students have been dramatically scaled down.

Enrolling sufficient numbers of students is another barrier that is not easily overcome. All the providers we interviewed offered voluntary programs for students; hence, site administrators needed to convince students (or their parents) that attending in the summer was worthwhile. Reported challenges to enrolling students in the voluntary programs we studied included a lack of advance marketing, recruiters who were not incentivized, and a lack of transportation.

Some program administrators reported waiting for spring state test results to determine who needed summer school and who they should try to recruit. However, by the time these test results were available, many families had already made summer plans. Many providers started to recruit for the next summer the day after the current summer program ended.

Interviewees also reported that the incentives offered to recruiters made a difference in enrollment levels. In some sites, recruiting was the responsibility of each school's principal, even though the principal was not necessarily involved in the summer program. In cases in which principals had no involvement with the summer program, interviewees reported uneven motivation to recruit students. Recruiters (principals, teachers, and district officials) who recruited early and used multiple avenues for recruiting reportedly had more success. Reported recruiting mechanisms included

- print advertising
- radio advertising

- advertising at community meetings, summer learning fairs, and even grocery stores
- targeted recruiting of students living in housing projects
- door-to-door recruiting
- phone calls to parents
- student and teacher focus groups
- CBO recruiting among after-school program attendees.

Some targeted middle school students by emphasizing enrichment opportunities: Enticing students into a program with fencing, kayaking, and arts opportunities seemed more likely to pay off than highlighting the opportunities for more mathematics and reading development.

Most of the providers we interviewed offered transportation for their students to the summer learning program, via either a school or city bus. In some districts, like Dallas, buses picked up students at their home schools rather than at their homes. Providers that did not offer transportation believed that the lack of it was a significant challenge to enrollment. Some providers, such as the city of Portland and the Minneapolis Public Schools, believed that offering a city bus pass provided students with an additional incentive to enroll in the program.

Quality Program Components

In our interviews, providers described what supported and challenged their efforts to ensure that students' summer learning experiences were high-quality. Our study did not specifically ask about the quality of the programs, neither did we attempt to measure quality. Instead, we allowed interviewees to reference their own definitions of quality. In so doing, some interviewees responded that they adhered to the National Summer Learning Association's quality standards (National Summer Learning Association, undated[b]). In general, their responses indicate that providers perceive individualized instruction that engages students as a key component of a quality program. The challenges to realizing this vision centered on the teachers and overall program funding.

Interviewees described several challenges that threatened the quality of the teachers providing instruction in their programs. Some expressed concern about having to hire teachers with the greatest seniority due to local contract requirements. Others stressed that, even when they thought they had selected the "right" teachers, some reverted to "old habits" of teaching that clashed with the interviewees' vision of an engaging learning environment. Indeed, we observed many different teaching styles across classes within a district. Some of the teacher interviewees complained about the quality of the teacher aides in their classes. For instance, in many programs, college students or other nonlicensed teachers are hired to supplement instruction; in some cases, interviewees questioned the value added by these teacher aides.

Inadequate funding threatened quality in at least two ways. In Minneapolis, summer program leaders lamented that they could not afford to purchase the curriculum that they wanted to use in each grade level. Other interviewees reported struggling to maintain small class sizes in the face of diminishing funding and access to facilities. Some providers, including the Pittsburgh Public Schools, questioned whether the amount they were spending to maintain a very low student-to-instructor ratio was worth the investment.

In Chapter Three, we summarized both evidence-based and expert-recommended recommendations on quality components of summer learning programs. Here, we align our field-work findings to those recommendations.

Smaller Class Sizes and Differentiated Instruction

As is recommended in the literature, all the providers' class sizes were reportedly smaller than they were during the school year. This reduced the ratio of students to teachers and drove up program costs, but it allowed greater differentiation of instruction. In addition to reducing the size of the class, many programs provided additional adults who could pull children out of the classroom who were in need of focused one-on-one time for learning.

High-Quality Instruction

Providers enacted several strategies to ensure effective instruction. As mentioned earlier, some interviewees developed mechanisms for recruiting teachers whom they thought would be well suited for their summer learning programs. Interviewees reported looking for teachers who would be motivated to teach students using a more active learning approach than was typical during the school year. Some districts and private providers selected teachers through an application process that required answers to essay questions. Others required teachers to develop and, in some cases, deliver mock lesson plans. Others only hired teachers who had taught in a high-performing school, as defined by the program administrators. Finally, others strove to hire teachers with backgrounds similar to those of their students so that the teachers could serve as role models.

Most of the summer learning programs we studied used very structured curricula, which is a strategy often used in an attempt to overcome variation in teacher effectiveness. The administrators we interviewed across sites and programs noted that there simply was not time to allow teachers to develop or even tailor the classroom curriculum. Many teachers reported appreciating the structure and the fact that the books and materials were delivered in time for the program to begin as planned. Many of the curricula were project- or theme-based, which is not at odds with a high degree of structure.

All the programs provided some training to teachers, typically for two to five days and focused on curriculum. Some teachers in the programs with four or more days of training argued that they did not need this much time for training and would have preferred to have more time familiarizing themselves with the classroom, school, and coordinators and aides with whom they would be working. Both private and district providers had hired instructional coaches to model instruction and provide ongoing support for teachers.

Aligned School-Year and Summer Curricula

Almost all providers tailored their programs to the state standards, at the very least and, in most cases, to the district's school-year curriculum. In Minneapolis, the district department chairs designed the summer curriculum. In Pittsburgh, a summer program leader led teachers in designing a curriculum based on benchmark assessment content areas on which the students did not perform well, such as making inferences.

Engaging and Rigorous Programming

Some believed that engaging enrichment experiences were also part of a quality program, as summer learning should feel "different" from school-year instruction. Providers achieved this goal both by providing enrichment experiences (e.g., fencing, kayaking, swimming) and by designing or selecting academic curricula that differed from that offered during the school year. In Pittsburgh, for example, the curriculum included the use of several different board games and other activities.

Maximized Participation and Attendance

Research clearly demonstrates that students need to attend summer learning programs to benefit from them. Most providers we interviewed stated that attendance rates generally fell into one of two extremes: Students either attended their programs regularly or, if they showed up at all, attended rarely. Unfortunately, providers noted that the lowest-performing students were the most likely to be absent.

Interviewees reported several strategies for maximizing attendance, most of which we also found in our review of the literature. Most providers reported that their main strategy for maintaining attendance was simply providing an engaging experience that the students would want to return to the following day. As noted by a representative of Classroom, Inc., "It is the program that keeps them attending." Others provided prizes on Fridays to students who had perfect attendance for the week. A few of the district-based programs and many of the private-provider programs we studied had instituted attendance policies, under which a student who had three unexcused absences would be expelled. These attendance policies were more likely to be enforced in programs for which there were wait lists, such as the Aim High programs in San Francisco and the Summer Scholar programs in Denver. Many programs that work with CBOs reimbursed these organizations based on the average daily attendance of students, thus incentivizing the CBOs to provide experiences that students enjoyed. Some programs actively developed mentor-mentee relationships between teachers and students in the hope that students would want to spend more time with the teachers. Finally, some of the private providers selected students strategically, offering placement to those who were from stable families, for example, or requiring student applicants to write essays as a way to demonstrate motivation to attend the program.

Sufficient Duration

Dosage varied across the programs, ranging from five to six hours a day, four to five days a week, and five to six weeks in total. All the programs provided dosage levels above the 80-hour recommendation of McLaughlin and Pitcock (2009) but below Winship et al.'s (2005) recommendation of eight weeks for five days a week and nine hours a day. As discussed earlier, at least one provider wants to expand its program but is concerned about teacher burnout and facilities constraints.

Involved Parents

The literature recommends involving parents, both to ensure high attendance rates and to reinforce learning in the home. To accomplish the former goal, many providers required parents to sign attendance pledges, called home when a child was absent, or required a small enrollment fee. To accomplish the latter goal, some providers invited parents to visit the program, either to observe their children or to take their own classes, or visited parents at home to talk about their children's progress in the program.

Evaluations of Effectiveness

The literature recommends regular evaluations of summer learning programs. Many providers conducted formative evaluations of students during the summer. For example, BELL has a weekly evaluation tool that it uses to quickly assess student learning and provide feedback to teachers. The Summer Scholars program in Denver conducts pre- and post-assessments, grouping students based on their performance. Some of the private providers also evaluated teachers throughout the summer and provided feedback based on the evaluation. Some district providers noted that they were prevented by union contract from evaluating teachers during the summer. Evaluations of the impact of summer learning programs on performance during the school year, as measured by performance on benchmark examinations or state assessments, were less common. Interviewees did report that students gained skills during the summer, based on pre- and post-tests, and were more likely than comparison groups to stay in school through graduation. However, interviewees were struggling to demonstrate to district and other leaders that the spring-to-fall gains they observed led to gains on state test scores. In many cases, students may gain over the summer but not enough to achieve proficiency on state tests. In other cases, even if students' test scores do rise, district researchers are unable to attribute that gain to the summer learning program, given everything that happens in a district between the fall and the spring, when state tests are administered.

Lessons on Where and How to Offer Programs

Our fieldwork provides some evidence of advantages to offering summer learning opportunities in districts. As described earlier, four of the five sites we visited provided programming in schools in the city's school district, as did many of the providers we interviewed by phone. Working from within a district enabled them to recruit students and teachers year-round. In Pittsburgh, program leaders conducted focus groups with students and teachers to simultaneously gather their preferences related to summer programming and market their plans. These program leaders also had easy access to district test-score data used to identify students' weaknesses. In Pittsburgh, district leaders built the literacy curriculum around those specific student weaknesses (e.g., text organization, point of view, headings, inferences). The specific programming may also be easier to align to the district curriculum when the program is offered by the district. In Minneapolis, for example, district mathematics and literacy coordinators specified a summer learning curriculum that would align with and support the school-year curriculum. Programs offered within a district also receive some degree of subsidization, as described in Chapter Four. Not only are they often able to use facilities at a discounted cost, but interviewees reported that parents are comfortable sending their students to schools that they are familiar with and, for elementary students, that have the right-sized desks, bathrooms, and so on, as opposed to college campuses and other community locations. (Other interviewees noted, however, that holding courses on college campuses exposed students to college and allowed them to feel comfortable in that space.) Finally, interviewees operating within a district noted that they could work year-round to garner support from, and develop plans with, other district departments, such as transportation, facilities, and food services. As noted earlier, these relationships were described as important in launching new summer learning programs.

Despite some evidence supporting district-based programs, there is also evidence to support the importance of partnering with CBOs. According to interviewees in Dallas, because a CBO and district provider jointly offered the summer program there, they were able to offer full-day rather than half-day programming, drawing more students than each had independently in prior years. Interviewees in San Francisco, Pittsburgh, and Minneapolis also attributed strong CBO-provided enrichment programming to attracting students to their programs in the first place and to keeping them engaged once enrolled.

Interviewees who worked outside the district also cautioned against a strictly district-based approach. Interviewees from local foundations in Pittsburgh worried that the program might become too bureaucratic over time. Interviewees from local foundations in San Francisco considered the lack of district funding for summer school an opportunity for the community to innovate in its summer learning strategies. But these same interviewees also believed that a higher proportion of students would be served by urban districts integrating summer learning into their own internal operations.

Conclusions

Providing summer learning programs that include quality program components is challenging, in terms of both developing such programs and maintaining and scaling them. Coordinating a new program for large numbers of students necessitates advance planning and dedication by motivated and qualified staff members who can execute the program vision. Maintaining these programs calls for leaders who are willing to prioritize or identify new funding for summer learning programs. For these programs to survive, districts need to value them.

Some of our interviewees questioned the value of summer programming. Some district representatives questioned the extent to which summer learning programs are worth the cost. Although the programs have clear potential to benefit students, this potential has been difficult to quantify. Most district leaders are concerned primarily with increasing the proportion of students in their districts who are scoring at the proficient level or above on state assessments. It may be unrealistic to expect dramatic state assessment score gains from participating in summer learning programs, particularly if the performance level of students is below basic when they start the program. On the other hand, it may simply be that districts do not have the methodological tools to detect such effects.

But there are district leaders who do believe in the importance and efficacy of their summer learning programs. Programs offered by districts in partnership with CBOs may attract the greatest proportion of students who could benefit from summer learning programs and may also develop a broad funding base. New funders, such as city governments and community foundations, may be attracted to these programs if they result in outcomes that appeal to them, such as keeping students safe in the summer or reducing delinquent behaviors. Districts can also reduce costs by focusing on the lowest-performing students or schools. We note, however, that the lowest-performing students may be two or three years below grade level, so dramatic results on state exams may not be apparent. However, participating in summer programs in early elementary grades may stop students from falling so far behind grade level in the first place.

Furthermore, partnering with CBOs to provide engaging enrichment activities was reported by our interviewees as central to attracting youth to the programs. Getting students to attend is obviously critical. Our interviewees agreed with the general literature that students will benefit only if they regularly attend the summer learning program. Unfortunately, none of the programs we studied was capturing all of its low-performing or high-need students. Although some programs were serving half of their target populations, none was serving the majority of these students.

The biggest threat to the quality of the programs we studied was enrolling a significant proportion of students and maintaining their attendance over the course of the summer program. Other program components, such as duration, class size, teachers, training, and curriculum, appeared to align with the evidence on quality components.

Districts and others launching summer learning programs will note that providing these quality components is feasible, albeit challenging. Challenges can be overcome by leaders who can dedicate and find funding for summer learning programs and ensure that qualified staff dedicate time to early planning, early hiring, and early recruiting for these programs.

CHAPTER SIX

Conclusions and Recommendations

Despite the evidence supporting summer learning programs and the recent attention they are receiving in the media and in policy debates, many large school districts do not offer such programs to their high-need students. Although there are many small summer learning programs in urban districts, few districts provide full-day academic and enrichment summer programs for their entire low-performing or high-need populations. Even when they do offer programs, as is the case in Minneapolis and in Albuquerque, it is difficult to attract more than half the students they are targeting.

There are several reasons that so many districts have not pursued summer programs for high-need students. The first is cost. Summer programming represents additional cost in a time of severe shortfalls in state education budgets. In fact, there are signs that summer learning programs are declining rather than growing. U.S. Secretary of Education Arne Duncan recently reported to Congress that survey estimates show that almost a third of school administrators plan to cut summer programming (Duncan, 2010). Second, our interviews pointed to several logistical challenges to developing and maintaining these programs, including developing consistent expectations and buy-in from multiple district departments and, in some cases, CBOs.

Third, there are limited data on the cost-effectiveness of summer learning programs. Given the challenges of funding and implementing a new program, district leaders need evidence that these programs can work for large numbers of low-performing students in urban districts and that they are worth the cost compared to other investments during the school year. There are not enough studies on large-scale summer learning programs to provide evidence that urban districts' students make achievement gains commensurate with the district's investment, and very few studies have assessed student outcomes over multiple, consecutive summers.

In this monograph, we synthesized what is known about the value of summer learning programs so that policymakers can learn from the most rigorous studies in the field. These studies have shown that vacation from school results in lost knowledge and skills and that this loss is particularly high for certain students. While all students lose some ground in mathematics, low-income students lose more ground in reading while their higher-income peers may even gain. Low-achieving students from all income levels need more time on task to achieve at the same performance levels as their peers and would benefit from summer programming. Lost ground in the summer is not made up during the school year, and this loss contributes to the achievement gap between low-income students and their more affluent peers. School-year efforts alone may be unsuccessful in closing this achievement gap.

Research also demonstrates that students can benefit in several ways from summer learning programs: They can master material that they did not learn during the previous school year, reverse summer learning loss, and even achieve learning gains. In all these ways, summer learning programs targeted to low-income students can help close the achievement gap that has been attributed, at least in part, to cumulative learning loss during the summers and that has been shown to be steeper for low-income students than for others. Longitudinal studies indicate that the effects of summer learning programs endure for at least two years after participation.

We have also summarized what studies have shown (and not shown) about the costs of summer programs, and we have added to that literature with an analysis of our own. Based on our sample, we demonstrated that summer learning programs can be less expensive than educating students during the school year, that they are less costly to districts than they are to external providers, that there are multiple funding options from public and private sources, and that districts that have a long history of sustaining these programs have cultivated relationships with CBOs, local politicians, and city agencies.

The ability to develop partnerships among school districts, government organizations, philanthropic organizations, CBOs, and families may affect the quality of the program as well. Each of these organizations has a set of resources and skills that can build sustainable summer learning programs. Districts can offer students, teachers, student data, facilities, central office management, transportation, food services, and curricular experts. CBOs can offer deep content knowledge in certain areas and can provide enrichment opportunities that go far beyond what is typically provided in schools. Nondistrict, national summer learning providers have vast experience in creating engaging summer academic programs that maximize attendance. Cities can offer funds, and they have an existing interest in keeping youth safe and engaged during the summer months. Local funders can bring additional resources to these programs. Partnerships can maximize resources and expertise to support quality and sustainment.

Recommendations for Districts and Providers

Districts and communities must decide for themselves whether the potential value of these programs is worth their investment. But the existing research and our analysis suggest that summer learning programs should be seriously considered within the context of student needs and available resources. We offer a set of recommendations for districts and other providers that want to invest in summer learning programs. Specifically, we recommend that districts and providers invest in staffing and planning for summer learning programs, actively incorporate practices that will help ensure the success of programs, and maximize the benefits of partnerships and a variety of funding sources.

Invest in Highly Qualified Staff and Early Planning

Developing high-quality summer learning programs can be challenging. We found that providers that succeeded in developing a well-structured program that attracted students to enroll and attend had high-quality, dedicated staff with time devoted to planning and programming. Planning began early in the school year. Early planning allowed programs to conduct early hiring (thereby maximizing their teacher recruiting pool) and early recruiting (thereby maximizing student enrollment).

Embed Promising Practices into Summer Learning Programs

Research shows that a number of practices are associated with improved student outcomes, such as smaller class sizes, involving parents, providing individualized instruction, and maximizing students' attendance. Other best practices include providing structures that support high-quality instruction, aligning the school year and summer curricula, including content beyond remediation, and tracking effectiveness. Providers also need to adopt strategies for attracting students to these programs to ensure value for their investment, such as print and radio advertising; advertising at community meetings, summer learning fairs, and even grocery stores; targeted recruiting of students living in housing projects, including door-to-door recruiting and phone calls to parents; student and teacher focus groups; and CBO recruiting among students in their after-school programs.

Consider Partnerships When Developing Summer Learning Programs

Partnerships may enable the creation and sustainment of high-quality voluntary summer learning programs. We found benefits from partnerships between school districts and CBOs that included lower costs, a wider variety of programming options, and more varied funding sources. However, a number of other partnerships may be beneficial, as several types of organizations have an interest in promoting summer learning experiences for youth—districts, CBOs, private summer learning providers, cities, and local funders. Each of these organizations has a set of resources and skills that can help build sustainable summer learning programs. We encourage leaders to consider all local resources and build appropriate partnerships when developing these programs.

Think Creatively About Funding

There are several pots of funding from which districts can draw to support summer learning programs. Researchers have documented, for example, more than 100 programs that can support summer learning. The National Summer Learning Association provides guidelines for funding summer learning programs on its website. Providers should also consider local funders, such as city governments and community foundations, which may be attracted to these programs if they result in outcomes that appeal to them, such as keeping students safe in the summer or reducing delinquent behaviors. This monograph provides other funding ideas, such as hiring AmeriCorps students and hiring teachers who need administrative hours to serve as summer site coordinators. Partnering with local CBOs can also result in economies of scale, as noted earlier.

Recommendations for Policymakers and Funders

Finally, we offer recommendations for policymakers and funders who are interested in supporting summer learning programs: Extend the research base on the efficacy of summer learning programs and support stable funding for new and existing programs.

Extend the Research Base

Although research has established the efficacy of summer learning programs, it has not tested several aspects of such programs when offered to large numbers of low-performing students in urban settings. Rigorous, longitudinal research on large programs would provide valuable information to policymakers and practitioners. In particular, we make the following recommendations:

- Conduct randomized controlled trials of programs designed to maximize attendance that compare treated to nontreated students over multiple years.
- Conduct studies that include multiple outcomes beyond academic performance: secondary academic outcomes, such as school attendance and graduation rates, and nonacademic outcomes, such as reductions in juvenile delinquency, improved nutrition, and increases in exercise. Including a range of outcomes will help motivate other stakeholders, such as city governments, to support or fund summer learning programs.
- Conduct studies that examine whether programs can be constructed to attract high-levels of participation in multiple, consecutive years of programming. If so, the studies should evaluate the effects of consecutive years of participation on a range of student outcomes.
- Conduct studies of the cost-effectiveness of summer learning programs to help district leaders and other policymakers consider how best to invest in improving education.

Support Consistent Funding Sources for Summer Learning Programs

A key obstacle to providing summer learning programs is a lack of stable funding. Policymakers at the federal, state, and local levels can work to provide funding for summer programming by specifying that existing funding targeted to high-need youth can be used for summer programming, by establishing new funding for programs, and by fundraising for summer programming. The school district officials whom we spoke with who run summer learning programs independently confirmed the importance of support from the superintendent, local politicians, and local foundations.

Provide Clear Guidance Regarding the Use of Scarce Funds

District leaders described the difficulty of braiding multiple funding sources together, given the restrictions and requirements associated with each source of funds. State policymakers could support district efforts by providing clear guidance on how federal and state funds can be combined to support summer programs.

APPENDIX

Approach to Cost Estimates for Summer Learning Programs

Data Collection and Cost Categories

A total of seven programs shared data with us. We conducted semistructured phone interviews with each provider, seeking cost detail for the most recent fiscal year for 22 categories of costs. When probing for costs, we first provided examples for each category, since the terminology is not uniform across programs.[1] Specifically, we requested cost detail about major cost ingredients, such as instructional staff, administrative staff, benefits, staff development, classroom materials, food, transportation, facilities, insurance, and contracted services. Within these categories, we solicited information about direct expenditures and in-kind contributions. We also sought information about each program's number, qualifications, and hours of volunteers. "Hidden costs," such as volunteerism and subsidized space, which are not direct monetary expenditures, nevertheless contribute to the overall economic cost of a program and would be costs that another provider would incur were it to replicate the given summer program. However, no provider we interviewed tracked information about the number, qualifications, *and* hours of volunteers, so we uniformly excluded this cost category. With one exception, each provider indicated minimal or no use of volunteers. Nevertheless, the exclusion of this in-kind cost category from the estimates is a limitation of the analysis.

A number of the summer learning programs did not possess data for certain cost categories. For example, Provider A (an externally led program) relies on its host school districts to cover the costs of meals for Provider A's participants, and, as such, it does not track those costs as part of its program. To account for the differences in each program's data collection, we reported in our discussion of costs several estimates on a per-slot, per-hour basis that successively include one additional feature (see Figure 4.2 in Chapter Four). We showed those estimates only for programs with features common to each; for example, estimates that include transportation are shown only for those

[1] For example, when soliciting total expenditures on central office staff, we asked for the combined total expenditures on salaries and benefits for all staff, excluding consultants and subcontractors (data on which were collected in a separate category). For providers that operated both summer school and after-school programming, we asked the providers to apportion the full year of salaries and benefits for the time devoted to summer school planning or administration.

programs that offered that service and where data were available about that cost. By iteratively adding in the cost of single program elements to the successive per-slot estimates, we could also identify which features accounted for the greatest proportion of the variation in costs across the providers.

Funds for services such as instruction, transportation, facilities, and nutrition are often difficult for summer program administrators to capture when they are tracked in entirely different budgets within a district. It is also difficult to track the actual expenditures for a particular program in individual schools. Many districts, for example, conduct staff-based budgeting by determining the number of teachers allocated to a given school based on the number of enrolled students (e.g., one FTE teacher for every 25 students) (Roza, 2010). After drawing up the total number of teachers in a school, a district budget office then multiplies the total number of FTE teachers by the average lead teacher salary in the district to come up with the total cost for lead teachers in a given school. This process may under- or overrepresent the actual expenditures on lead teachers in a given school if it employs teachers who are systematically more expensive than the districtwide average (as schools with the most experienced and most degreed teachers do) or less expensive than the districtwide average (i.e., as schools that hire the least-experienced or least-degreed teachers do).

To develop comprehensive estimates of costs for district-led programs in each of the three districts sampled, we sought to obtain data from each respective department with responsibility for instruction, meals, transit, and facilities. Nevertheless, these departments often provided prorated estimates derived from dividing aggregate expenditures by average daily attendance in a program. As such, they were the best estimates available of the true expenditures that the district made to provide the summer program. Absent better information, it is difficult to discern whether differences between district-led and externally led programs reflect true differences in practice (e.g., economies of scale or efficiencies) or whether they are an artifact of different accounting practices.

Adjustment to National Average Prices

To adjust for regional differences in prices, all figures in this report are adjusted to national average prices in the United States according to the Comparable Wage Index (CWI), available from the National Center for Education Statistics (Taylor, Glander, and Fowler, 2007). The CWI measures the systematic, regional variations in the salaries of college graduates who are not educators. We used the CWI to adjust district-level (or state-level) finance data to make better comparisons across summer learning program expenditures. Since the CWI is a labor cost index, it is not designed to adjust for regional differences in the cost of materials or other nonlabor costs associated with summer learning programs. However, since labor-related costs account for the majority of overall educational costs, we used a labor-based index instead of an index based on a "market basket" approach (one that assesses regional differences in costs for a given set of goods).

To account for inflation, we adjusted nominal dollars into 2009 or 2010 real dollars using the Consumer Price Index (CPI), which is the most common way to measure inflation (Fowler and Monk, 2001). If inflation in the education section differs from the rate of inflation found in other sectors, the CPI becomes a less precise tool for adjustment to education prices. However, each inflation index has limitations. For simplicity and for comparability with other reports in which CPI was used, we employed it here.

Per-Slot Estimates

Cost per *enrollee* is the total cost of the program divided by its total enrollment (Grossman et al., 2009). Total enrollment is usually higher than the attendance on a typical day—especially for summer learning programs in which attendance rates can be quite low. Cost per *slot* is the total cost of the program divided by average daily attendance, i.e., the typical number of students present on any given day. Especially in the case of summer school, expressing costs by slot better represents the true costs of a program per individual, since it divides the cost of services by the typical number of recipients who consumed them. Put another way, the cost per slot represents the cost of adding one more student who attends for the entire duration of the program. We believe that this is the fairest way to compare the costs of programs, since it takes into account the variation in student attendance across programs. We also believe that it is the most reasonable way to present a range of summer learning program costs, because it takes into account elevated rates of absenteeism that summer learning programs often encounter relative to compulsory schooling during the academic year. However, since many school districts budget for summer programs based on projected total enrollments rather than total slots, we also report the costs per enrollee in this appendix.

Estimating the Cost Effect of the Student-to-Instructor Ratio

The student-to-instructor ratio was the program element most highly correlated with cost, followed by differences in minimum teacher qualifications. Although the public school districts hired certified teachers for at least the morning (academic) portion of the summer program, they typically hired fewer instructors per student than the other programs. Thus, the extra cost associated with hiring certified teachers was offset by the savings realized from the increased student-to-instructor ratio. For example, Providers D and E placed a certified teacher as a lead instructor in each classroom but did not pair them with aides in every case. Almost all the other programs, by contrast, blended their instructional staff by pairing certified or lead/mentor teachers (usually a year-round teacher in either a public or private school) with assistant teachers enrolled in either high school or college.

Provider's staffing structures and ratios varied considerably. Provider D paid approximately $25 per classroom teacher per hour (depending on the grade level, one teacher for every 17 to one for every 29 students) in addition to placing one English for speakers of other languages and one special education teacher per site. It also contracted with the county's recreation department and an arts and humanities organization for the afternoon programming offered at a subset of its Title I elementary schools (at a lower staff cost). Provider F, on the other hand, paid summer stipends equal to a rate of $25 or $36 per hour per certified classroom teacher per summer (one for every 20 students) and then, for electives, hired high school or college students as camp counselors for $15 per hour per summer (one for every eight students) and afternoon facilitators at $23 per hour (about one for every 33 students). The camp counselors worked all day and thus worked with the certified teachers in the morning and were under the supervision of facilitators in the afternoon. Depending on the region and the individual's experience level, Provider A hired classroom teachers (one for every ten students) at rates ranging from $25 to $42 per hour and then hired assistant teachers (one for every students) at $10–$16 per hour, along with one lead teacher per site at a rate of $2–$4 more per hour than regular classroom teachers. Provider B, meanwhile, placed one teacher and one assistant teacher in each classroom. Provider C hired two to four mentor teachers per site from top-tier schools in the community (public or private), and these mentor teachers floated across classrooms that were led by high school or college students at a ratio of one to every four students. In addition to the director and assistant director positions, Provider C hired a dean of faculty and a dean of students at each site to help oversee the program.

Calculating the Difference Between Summer and School-Year Costs

We found that summer programming offered by a district tends to be less expensive on a weekly per-pupil basis than education costs during the academic year. To draw this comparison, we converted the total per-summer, per-slot expenditures shown in Figure 4.1 in Chapter Four into a weekly per-slot cost for the three school district–led programs (Providers D, E, and F) and included imputed values for food, transportation, and facilities, since these are fully captured costs in districts' academic-year budgets, which is our point of comparison. We then collected data on total calendar year expenditures from 2009 for these same districts, subtracting their expenditures on the summer program in question. We divided these adjusted total district-level expenditures by the number of operational school weeks in the year (including holidays and professional development days) and the total number of enrollees multiplied by the average attendance rate in the district to develop a per-slot, per-week school-year cost.

Detailed Cost Estimates

Although we attempted to collect the complete set of expenditures associated with each program, many summer learning programs did not have data on certain costs. To account for the differences in the programs' data collection, we show only successive estimates in the following tables on a per-slot, per-hour basis for programs with features common to each. We also impute costs for three commonly missing or partially subsidized activities—transportation, food, and facilities—that we then uniformly apply to each program to derive total estimates, as shown in Figure 4.1 in Chapter Four.

Table A.1 shows a cost breakdown for all our categories of core expenses for all providers on a per-slot basis. Although we collected cost data from six classroom-based providers, they in fact operate eight distinct programs. Provider C is a national program with affiliates that either are hosted by private schools or are themselves nonprofit organizations. The nonhosted affiliates that are nonprofit organizations bear a greater proportion of the total economic cost of the program than the affiliates hosted at private schools, which subsidize the costs of administration, facilities, and food. To isolate the unsubsidized costs of the program, we separately report average costs for hosted sites (i.e., affiliates operated by and at private school campuses) and the average costs for nonhosted sites where nonprofit organizations run the summer program. We broke Provider D into two parts in Table 4.2 in Chapter Four to reflect the distinct programmatic differences between its morning academic program (funded by one source) and its afternoon program, which serves only a portion of the morning students (and is funded by another source).

Table A.2 shows totals for additional costs, such as meals and transportation per slot per summer and per slot per hour. Table A.3 shows these cost categories on a per-enrollee rather than per-slot basis.

Table A.1
Cost Categories on a per-Slot, per-Summer Basis

	Externally Led Programs				District-Led Programs				Books-Only Program
Category	**Provider A**	**Provider B**	**Provider C (hosted sites)**	**Provider C (nonhosted sites)**	**Provider D (academic portion)**	**Provider D (recreational portion)**	**Provider E**	**Provider F**	**Provider G**
Central (national/district) office expenses ($)									
Salaries + benefits	466	262	***	***	23	39	39	262	126
Contracted services	51	45	***	***	0	0	41	0	32
Facilities	103	21	***	***	—	—	—	—	—
Travel to oversee sites	14	26	***	***	NA	NA	NA	NA	4
Grants to affiliates	NA	132	NA	NA	NA	NA	NA	NA	NA
Fundraising	6	0	***	***	NA	NA	NA	NA	NA
Total national-level costs	701	486	303	303	23	39	80	262	162
Site-level expenses per pupil ($)									
Administrator/support service salaries	332	368	474	649	80	32	44	128	NA
Teacher salaries	496	1,159	663	648	279	0	518	976	NA
Benefits and taxes	150	149	307	441	52	3	114	***	NA
Staff development	14	161	61	66	0	0	25	0	NA
Instructional materials	73	80	34	23	11	1	121	82	39
Administrative materials	11	93	104	131	17	—	16	143	22
Trips for children	26	69	23	24	NA	0	0	0	NA
Outreach	0	23	81	101	0	0	0	0	NA
Contracted services	0	0	40	103	0	267	38	845	NA

Table A.1—Continued

	Externally Led Programs				District-Led Programs				Books-Only Program
Category	**Provider A**	**Provider B**	**Provider C (hosted sites)**	**Provider C (nonhosted sites)**	**Provider D (academic portion)**	**Provider D (recreational portion)**	**Provider E**	**Provider F**	**Provider G**
Facilities	113	—	16	186	20	27	—	—	NA
Meals	—	130	128	66	66	34	54	348	22
Transportation	—	151	110	145	15	6	60	338	NA
Other	50	110	137	94	0	7	0	25	NA
Dues	NA	NA	61	40	NA	NA	NA	NA	NA
Total site-level costs	1,263	2,493	2,240	2,719	540	376	992	2,885	83
Total central and site-level costs[a] ($)	1,964	2,979	2,543	3,022	563	349	1,073	3,147	245

SOURCE: Authors' tabulations from phone interviews with and data from program providers.

NOTE: Costs have been adjusted to 2009 dollars to account for inflation and national average costs to account for regional differences in the price of labor. *** = Cost included in another category. — = Not available from provider. NA = Cost not applicable to program.

[a] Total costs do not include all of the same categories, for which cost data are sometimes missing.

Table A.2
Incremental Additional Costs of Ingredients on a per-Slot Basis

	Externally Led Programs				District-Led Programs				Books-Only Program
Category	Provider A	Provider B	Provider C (hosted sites)	Provider C (nonhosted sites)	Provider D (academic portion)	Provider D (recreational portion)	Provider E	Provider F	Provider G
Per slot per summer ($)									
A: central office + site operating costs only	874	1,022	844	886	51	39	281	1,357	245
B: A + instructor salaries	1,370	2,181	1,507	1,534	330	263	799	2,333	245
C: B + administrator/ support salaries	1,851	2,698	2,288	2,625	462	292	958	2,461	245
D: C + meals	—	2,828	2,416	2,691	528	321	1,012	2,809	NA
E: D + transportation	—	2,979	2,527	2,836	543	326	1,073	3,147	NA
F: E + facilities (all services included)	—	—	—	3,022	563	349	—	—	NA
Per slot per hour ($)									
A: central office + site operating costs only	5	6	6	6	1	0	2	8	NA
B: A + instructor salaries	8	12	11	11	4	3	7	14	NA
C: B + administrator/ support salaries	11	15	16	19	6	4	8	15	NA
D: C + meals	—	16	17	19	7	4	8	17	NA
E: D + transportation	—	17	18	20	7	4	9	19	NA
F: E + facilities (all services included)	—	—	—	22	7	4	—	—	NA

SOURCE: Authors' tabulations from phone interviews with and data from program providers.

NOTE: Costs have been adjusted to 2009 dollars to account for inflation and national average costs to account for regional differences in the price of labor. — = Cost not provided where cost of ingredient not available from the provider. NA = Not applicable to program.

Table A.3
Cost Categories on a per-Enrollee, per-Summer Basis

	Externally Led Programs				District-Led Programs				Books-Only Program
Category	**Provider A**	**Provider B**	**Provider C (hosted sites)**	**Provider C (nonhosted sites)**	**Provider D (academic portion)**	**Provider D (recreational portion)**	**Provider E**	**Provider F**	**Provider G**
Total enrollments	3,130	1,689	2,466	456	7,552	945	5,750	1,900	370
Total slots (typical number of students present per day)	2,661	1,571	2,211	409	6,510	794	2,000	1,300	370
Attendance rate (%)	85	93	89	89	86	84	83	68	NA
Central (national/district) office expenses ($)									
Salaries + benefits	396	244	***	***	20	33	33	179	126
Contracted services	43	42	***	***	0	0	34	0	32
Facilities	88	19	***	***	—	—	—	—	—
Travel to oversee sites	12	25	***	***	NA	NA	NA	NA	4
Grants to affiliates	NA	123	NA	NA	NA	NA	NA	0	NA
Fundraising	5	0	***	***	NA	NA	NA	NA	NA
Total national-level costs	596	452	272	272	20	33	67	179	162
Site-level expenses per pupil ($)									
Administrator/support service salaries	282	342	474	649	69	27	37	88	NA
Teacher salaries	421	1,078	663	648	240	0	433	668	NA
Benefits and taxes	127	139	307	441	45	2	96	***	NA
Staff development	12	150	61	66	0	0	21	0	NA
Instructional materials	62	74	34	23	9	1	101	56	39

Table A.3—Continued

	Externally Led Programs				District-Led Programs				Books-Only Program
Category	Provider A	Provider B	Provider C (hosted sites)	Provider C (nonhosted sites)	Provider D (academic portion)	Provider D (recreational portion)	Provider E	Provider F	Provider G
Administrative materials	9	87	104	131	15	—	14	98	22
Trips for children	22	64	23	24	0	0	0	0	NA
Outreach	0	22	81	101	0	0	0	0	NA
Contracted services	0	0	40	103	0	224	32	578	NA
Facilities	96	—	16	186	17	22	—	—	NA
Meals	—	121	128	66	57	29	54	238	22
Transportation	—	140	110	145	13	5	50	231	NA
Other	42	102	137	94	0	6	0	17	NA
Dues	NA	NA	61	40	NA	NA	NA	NA	NA
Total site-level costs	1,074	2,319	2,240	2,719	465	316	837	1,974	83
Total central and site-level costs[a] ($)	1,670	2,770	2,512	2,990	485	349	904	2,153	245

SOURCE: Authors' tabulations from phone interviews with and data from program providers.

NOTE: Costs have been adjusted to 2009 dollars to account for inflation and national average costs to account for regional differences in the price of labor. *** = Cost included in another category. — = Not available from provider. NA = Cost not applicable to program.

[a] Total costs do not include all of the same categories because cost data were sometimes missing.

References

Aarnoutse, Cor, Jan van Leeuwe, Marinus Voeten, and Han Oud, "Development of Decoding, Reading Comprehension, Vocabulary and Spelling During the Elementary School Years," *Reading and Writing*, Vol. 14, Nos. 1–2, March 2001, pp. 61–89.

Adams, Jack A., *Human Memory*, New York: McGraw-Hill, 1967.

Alexander, Karl L., and Doris R. Entwisle, "Schools and Children at Risk," in Alan Booth and Judith F. Dunn, eds., *Family-School Links: How Do They Affect Educational Outcomes?* Mahwah, N.J.: Erlbaum, 1996, pp. 67–89.

Alexander, Karl L., Doris R. Entwisle, and Linda Steffel Olson, "Schools, Achievement, and Inequality: A Seasonal Perspective," *Educational Evaluation and Policy Analysis*, Vol. 23, No. 2, June 2001, pp. 171–191.

———, "Lasting Consequences of the Summer Learning Gap," *American Sociological Review*, Vol. 72, No. 2, April 2007, pp. 167–180.

Allinder, Rose M., Lynn S. Fuchs, Douglas Fuchs, and Carol L. Hamlett, "Effects of Summer Break on Math and Spelling Performance as a Function of Grade Level," *The Elementary School Journal*, Vol. 92, No. 4, March 1992, pp. 451–460.

Allington, Richard L., Anne McGill-Franzen, Gregory Camilli, Lunetta Williams, Jennifer Graff, Jacqueline Zeig, Courtney Zmach, and Rhonda Nowak, "Addressing Summer Reading Setback Among Economically Disadvantaged Elementary Students," *Reading Psychology*, Vol. 31, No. 5, October 2010, pp. 411–427.

Arbreton, Amy, Jessica Sheldon, Molly Bradshaw, and Julie Goldsmith, with Linda Jucovy and Sarah Pepper, *Advancing Achievement: Findings from an Independent Evaluation of a Major After-School Initiative*, Philadelphia, Pa.: Public/Private Ventures, February 2008. As of May 10, 2011: http://www.ppv.org/ppv/publications/assets/225_publication.pdf

Aronson, Julie, Joy Zimmerman, and Lisa Carlos, *Improving Student Achievement by Extending School: Is It Just a Matter of Time?* San Francisco, Calif.: WestEd, 1998.

Baldwin, Robert D., Robert E. Cliborn, and Robert J. Foskett, *The Acquisition and Retention of Visual Aircraft Recognition Skills*, Alexandria, Va.: U.S. Army Research Institute for the Behavioral and Social Sciences, Technical Report TR-76-A4, November 1976.

Beckett, Megan K., *Current-Generation Youth Programs: What Works, What Doesn't, and At What Cost?* Santa Monica, Calif.: RAND Corporation, OP-215-GJ, 2008. As of May 10, 2011: http://www.rand.org/pubs/occasional_papers/OP215.html

Belfield, Clive R., and Henry M. Levin, *The Return on Investment for Improving California's High School Graduation Rate*, Santa Barbara, Calif.: California Dropout Research Project, University of California, Santa Barbara, Report No. 2, August 2007. As of April 22, 2011: http://www.cbcse.org/media/download_gallery/California%20Dropout%20Study%20Report%202FINAL.pdf

Bell, Susanne R., and Natalie Carrillo, "Characteristics of Effective Summer Learning Programs in Practice," *New Directions for Youth Development*, Vol. 2007, No. 114, Summer 2007, pp. 45–63.

Benefield, Kerry, "Most Sonoma County Districts Cutting School Days," *Press Democrat* (California), July 23, 2010. As of April 22, 2011: http://www.pressdemocrat.com/article/20100723/NEWS/100729715

Benson, James, and Geoffrey D. Borman, "Family, Neighborhood, and School Settings Across Seasons: When Do Socioeconomic Context and Racial Composition Matter for the Reading Achievement Growth of Young Children?" *Teacher's College Record*, Vol. 112, No. 5, 2010, pp. 1338–1390.

Bloom, Benjamin, *Human Characteristics and School Learning*, New York: McGraw-Hill, 1976.

Borman, Geoffrey, James Benson, and Laura Overman, "Families Schools and Summer Learning," *The Elementary School Journal*, Vol. 106, No. 2, November 2005, pp. 131–150.

Borman, Geoffrey D., and N. Maritza Dowling, "Longitudinal Achievement Effects of Multiyear Summer School: Evidence from the Teach Baltimore Randomized Field Trial," *Educational Evaluation and Policy Analysis*, Vol. 28, No. 1, March 2006, pp. 25–48.

Borman, Geoffrey, Michael Goetz, and N. Maritza Dowling, "Halting the Summer Achievement Slide: A Randomized Field Trial of the KindergARTen Summer Camp," *Journal of Education for Students Placed at Risk*, Vol. 14, No. 2, April 2009, pp. 133–147.

Boss, Suzie, and Jennifer Railsback, *Summer School Programs: A Look at the Research, Implications for Practice, and Program Sampler*, Portland, Oreg.: Northwest Regional Educational Laboratory, September 2002.

Brooks-Gunn, Jeanne, and Greg J. Duncan, "The Effects of Poverty on Children," *The Future of Children*, Vol. 7, No. 2, 1997, pp. 55–71.

Brown, Byron W., and Daniel H. Saks, "Measuring the Effects of Instructional Time on Student Learning: Evidence from the Beginning Teacher Evaluation Study," *American Journal of Education*, Vol. 94, No. 4, August 1986, pp. 480–500.

Bryk, Anthony S., and Stephan W. Raudenbush, "Toward a More Appropriate Conceptualization of Research on School Effects: A Three-Level Hierarchical Linear Model," *American Journal of Education*, Vol. 97, No. 1, November 1988, pp. 65–108.

Burkam, David T., Douglas D. Ready, Valerie E. Lee, and Laura F. LoGerfo, "Social-Class Differences in Summer Learning Between Kindergarten and First Grade: Model Specification and Estimation," *Sociology of Education*, Vol. 77, No. 1, January 2004, pp. 1–31.

Carroll, John, "A Model of School Learning," *Teachers College Record*, Vol. 64, No. 8, 1963, pp. 723–742.

———, "The Carroll Model: A 25-Year Retrospective and Prospective View," *Educational Researcher*, Vol. 18, No. 1, January 1989, pp. 26–31.

Chaplin, Duncan, and Jeffrey Capizzano, *Impacts of a Summer Learning Program: A Random Assignment Study of Building Educated Leaders for Life (BELL)*, Washington, D.C.: Urban Institute, 2006. As of April 22, 2011: http://www.urban.org/publications/411350.html

Child Care Bureau, *Using the Child Care and Development Fund to Support a System of Quality Improvement for School-Age Programs*, Washington, D.C., September 2009.

Conley, David T., and Kathryn C. Rooney, *Pennsylvania State Board of Education Costing-Out Study: Evidence Based Method*, Eugene, Oreg.: Educational Policy Improvement Center, August 2007.

Cooper, Graham, and John Sweller, "Effects of Schema Acquisition and Rule Automation on Mathematical Problem-Solving Transfer," *Journal of Educational Psychology*, Vol. 79, No. 4, December 1987, pp. 347–362.

Cooper, Harris, Kelly Charlton, Jeff C. Valentine, and Laura Muhlenbruck, with Geoffrey D. Borman, *Making the Most of Summer School: A Meta-Analytic and Narrative Review*, Monographs of the Society for Research in Child Development, Vol. 65, No. 1, Malden, Mass.: Blackwell Publishers, 2000.

Cooper, Harris, Barbara Nye, Kelly Charlton, James Lindsay, and Scott Greathouse, "The Effects of Summer Vacation on Achievement Test Scores: A Narrative and Meta-Analytic Review," *Review of Educational Research*, Vol. 66, No. 3, Fall 1996, pp. 227–268.

Cooper, Harris, Jeffrey C. Valentine, Kelly Charlton, and April Melson, "The Effects of Modified School Calendars on Student Achievement and on School and Community Attitudes," *Review of Educational Research*, Vol. 73, No. 1, Spring 2003, pp. 1–52.

Cotton, Kathleen, *Educational Time Factors*, Portland, Ore.: Northwest Regional Educational Laboratory, 1989.

Curry, Janice, *Summer Opportunity to Accelerate Reading (S.O.A.R.) Evaluation, 2001*, Austin, Tex.: Austin Independent School District, December 2001.

Denton, David R., *Summer School: Unfulfilled Promise*, Atlanta, Ga.: Southern Regional Education Board, 2002.

Dobbins-Harper, Dionne, and Soumya Bhat, *Finding Funding: A Guide to Federal Sources for Youth Programs*, Washington, D.C.: The Finance Project, 2007.

Downey, Douglas B., Paul T. von Hippel, and Beckett A. Broh, "Are Schools the Great Equalizer? Cognitive Inequality During the Summer Months and the School Year," *American Sociological Review*, Vol. 69, No. 5, October 2004, pp. 613–635.

Duncan, Arne, U.S. Secretary of Education, testimony before the Senate Appropriations Subcommittee on Labor, Health and Human Services, Education, and Related Agencies, regarding the fiscal year 2011 education budget, April 14, 2010. As of April 25, 2011: http://www2.ed.gov/news/speeches/2010/04/04142010.html

Entwisle, Doris R., and Karl L. Alexander, "Summer Setback: Race, Poverty, School Composition, and Mathematics Achievement in the First Two Years of School," *American Sociological Review*, Vol. 57, No. 1, February 1992, pp. 72–84.

———, "Winter Setback: School Racial Composition and Learning to Read," *American Sociological Review*, Vol. 59, No. 3, June 1994, pp. 446–460.

Fairchild, Ron, Jeff Smink, and Ashley B. Stewart, *It's Time for Summer: An Analysis of Recent Policy and Funding Opportunities*, New York: The Wallace Foundation, September 2009.

Fisher, Charles W., David C. Berliner, Nikola N. Filby, Richard Marliave, Leonard S. Cahen, and Marilyn M. Dishaw, "Teaching Behaviors, Academic Learning Time, and Student Achievement: An Overview," in Carolyn Denham and Ann Lieberman, eds., *Time to Learn: A Review of the Beginning Teacher Evaluation Study*, Sacramento, Calif.: California State Commission for Teacher Preparation and Licensing, 1980, pp. 7–32.

Fowler, William J., Jr., and David H. Monk, *A Primer for Making Cost Adjustments in Education*, Washington, D.C.: National Center for Education Statistics, NCES 2001-323, February 2001.

Freedberg, Louis, "Districts Cut School Year to Save Cash," *Sacramento Bee*, July 16, 2010, p. 1A.

Garlin, G. R., and T. E. Sitterley, *Degradation of Learned Skills: A Review and Annotated Bibliography*, Seattle, Wash.: Boeing, 1972.

Geary, David C., "Reflections of Evolution and Culture in Children's Cognition: Implications for Mathematical Development and Instruction," *American Psychologist*, Vol. 50, No. 1, January 1995, pp. 24–37.

Gettinger, Maribeth, "Effects of Maximizing Time Spent and Minimizing Time Needed for Learning on Pupil Achievement," *American Educational Research Journal*, Vol. 26, No. 1, March 1989, pp. 73–91.

Goetze, Linda D., and Cora L. Price, *An Evaluation of K–3 Plus Implementation, Progress, and Children's Learning in New Mexico*, Logan, Utah: Early Intervention Research Institute, Utah State University, Fall 2009.

Goldberg, Stephen L., Matthew Drillings, and J. Douglas Dressel, *Mastery Training: Effects on Skill Retention*, Alexandria, Va.: U.S. Army Research Institute for the Behavioral and Social Sciences, Technical Report 513, 1981.

Griffith, Michael, and Kyle Zinth, *Issues in Funding Summer School Programs*, Denver, Colo.: Education Commission of the States, 2009.

Grossman, Jean Baldwin, Christianne Lind, Cheryl Hayes, Jennifer McMaken, and Andrew Gersick, *The Cost of Quality Out-of-School-Time Programs*, New York: The Wallace Foundation, 2009.

Haertel, Geneva D., Herbert J. Walberg, and Thomas Weinstein, "The Psychological Models of Educational Performance: A Theoretical Synthesis of Constructs," *Review of Educational Research*, Vol. 53, No. 1, Spring 1983, pp. 75–91.

Hagman, Joseph D., *Effects of Training Schedule and Equipment Variety on Retention and Transfer of Maintenance Skill*, Alexandria, Va.: U.S. Army Research Institute for Behavioral and Social Sciences, Research Report 1309, 1980.

Harnischfeger, Annegret, and David E. Wiley, "The Teaching-Learning Process in Elementary Schools: A Synoptic View," *Curriculum Inquiry*, Vol. 6, No. 1, Fall 1976, pp. 5–43.

Harris, Douglas N., and Tim R. Sass, *What Makes for a Good Teacher and Who Can Tell?* New York: National Center for Analysis of Longitudinal Data in Education Research, Working Paper 30, 2009.

Hart, Betty, and Todd R. Risley, *Meaningful Differences in the Everyday Experience of Young American Children*, Baltimore, Md.: Brookes Publishing, 1995.

Hawley, Willis D., Susan Rosenholtz, Henry J. Goodstein, and Ted Hasselbring, "Good Schools: What Research Says About Improving Student Achievement," *Peabody Journal of Education*, Vol. 61, No. 4, Summer 1984, pp. iii–178.

Heyns, Barbara, *Summer Learning and the Effects of Schooling*, New York: Academic Press, 1978.

———, "Schooling and Cognitive Development: Is There a Season for Learning?" *Child Development*, Vol. 58, No. 5, October 1987, pp. 1151–1160.

Hill, Carolyn J., Howard S. Bloom, Alison Rebeck Black, and Mark W. Lipsey, *Empirical Benchmarks for Interpreting Effect Sizes in Research*, New York: MDRC, July 2007. As of April 13, 2011:
http://www.mdrc.org/publications/459/abstract.html

Jacob, Brian A., and Lars Lefgren, "Remedial Education and Student Achievement: A Regression-Discontinuity Design," *Review of Economics and Statistics*, Vol. 86, No. 1, February 2004, pp. 226–244.

Jencks, Christopher, and Meredith Phillips, "The Black-White Test Scope Gap: Why It Persists and What Can Be Done," *The Brookings Review*, Vol. 16, No. 2, Spring 1998, pp. 24–27.

Karweit, Nancy, "Should We Lengthen the School Term?" *Educational Researcher*, Vol. 14, No. 6, June 1985, pp. 9–15.

Karweit, Nancy, and Robert E. Slavin, "Time-on-Task: Issues of Timing, Sampling, and Definition," *Journal of Educational Psychology*, Vol. 74, No. 6, December 1982, pp. 844–851.

Ketterlin-Geller, Leanne R., David J. Chard, and Hank Fien, "Making Connections in Mathematics: Conceptual Mathematics Intervention for Low Performing Students," *Remedial and Special Education*, Vol. 29, No. 1, January–February 2008, pp. 33–45.

Kim, James S., "Effects of a Voluntary Summer Reading Intervention on Reading Achievement: Results from a Randomized Field Trial," *Educational Evaluation and Policy Analysis*, Vol. 28, No. 4, December 2006, pp. 335–355.

Kim, James S., and Jonathan Guryan, "The Efficacy of a Voluntary Summer Book Reading Intervention for Low-Income Latino Children from Language Minority Families," *Journal of Educational Psychology*, Vol. 102, No. 1, February 2010, pp. 20–31.

Kim, James S., and Thomas G. White, "Scaffolding Voluntary Summer Reading for Children in Grades 3 to 5: An Experimental Study," *Scientific Studies of Reading*, Vol. 12, No. 1, 2008, pp. 1–23.

Kim, Jimmy, "Summer Reading and the Ethnic Achievement Gap," *Journal of Education for Students Placed at Risk*, Vol. 9, No. 2, April 2004, pp. 169–188.

Lee, Valerie E., and David T. Burkham, *Inequality at the Starting Gate: Social Background Differences in Achievement as Children Begin School*, Washington, D.C.: Economic Policy Institute, 2002.

Lomax, Richard G., and William W. Cooley, "The Student Achievement–Instructional Time Relationship," paper presented at the annual meeting of the American Educational Research Association, San Francisco, Calif., April 1979.

Matsudaira, Jordan D., "Mandatory Summer School and Student Achievement," *Journal of Econometrics*, Vol. 142, No. 2, 2008, pp. 829–850.

McCombs, Jennifer Sloan, Sheila Nataraj Kirby, and Louis T. Mariano, *Ending Social Promotion Without Leaving Children Behind: The Case of New York City*, Santa Monica, Calif.: RAND Corporation, MG-894-NYCDOE, 2009. As of April 22, 2011:
http://www.rand.org/pubs/monographs/MG894.html

McLaughlin, Brenda, and Sarah Pitcock, *Building Quality in Summer Learning Programs: Approaches and Recommendations*, New York: The Wallace Foundation, 2009.

Monrad, Diane M., and John May, *Year 2000 Summer School in South Carolina: Program Description and Costs*, Columbia, S.C.: South Carolina Educational Policy Center, University of South Carolina, March 2001.

Murnane, Richard J., *The Impact of School Resources on the Learning of Inner City Children*, Cambridge, Mass.: Balinger Publishing Company, 1975.

National Center for Education Statistics, "Percentage of High School Dropouts Among Persons 16 Through 24 Years Old (Status Dropout Rate), by Income Level, and Percentage Distribution of Status Dropouts, by Labor Force Status and Educational Attainment: 1970 Through 2006," Table 106, *Digest of Education Statistics*, Washington, D.C.: Government Printing Office, 2007.

National League of Cities, *Financial Strategies to Support Citywide Systems of Out-of-School Time Programs*, Washington, D.C.: Institute for Youth, Education, and Families, 2009.

National Summer Learning Association, "Organizations and Districts," web page, undated(a). As of April 25, 2011:
http://www.summerlearning.org/?page=members

———, "Quality Standards," web page, undated(b). As of April 26, 2011:
http://www.summerlearning.org/?page=quality_standards

Naylor, James C., and George E. Briggs, *Long-Term Retention of Learned Skills: A Review of the Literature*, Canton, Ohio: Aerospace Medical Laboratory, Wright-Patterson Air Force Base, Technical Report 61-390, 1961.

Osborn, William C., Charlotte H. Campbell, and James H. Harris, *The Retention of Tank Crewman Skills*, Alexandria, Va.: U.S. Army Research Institute for Behavioral and Social Sciences, Research Report 1234, 1979.

Paris, Scott G., "Reinterpreting the Development of Reading Skills," *Reading Research Quarterly*, Vol. 40, No. 2, April–June 2005, pp. 184–202.

Prophet, Wallace W., *Long Term Retention of Flying Skills: A Review of the Literature*, Alexandria, Va.: Human Resources Research Organization, Report 46-35, 1977.

Relave, Nanette, and Margaret Flynn-Khan, *Using TANF to Finance Out-of-School Time Initiatives*, Washington, D.C.: The Finance Project, June 2007.

Roderick, Melissa, Mimi Engel, and Jenny Nagaoka, with Brian A. Jacobs, Sophie Deneger, Alex Orfel, Susan Stone, and Jen Bacon, *Ending Social Promotion: Results from Summer Bridge*, Chicago, Ill.: Consortium on Chicago School Research, University of Chicago, February 2003.

Rohrer, Doug, and H. Pashler, "Recent Research on Human Learning Challenges Conventional Instructional Strategies," *Educational Researcher*, Vol. 39, 2010, pp. 406–412.

Rohrer, Doug, and Kelli Taylor, "The Effects of Overlearning and Distributed Practice on the Retention of Mathematics Knowledge," *Applied Cognitive Psychology*, Vol. 20, No. 2, March 2006, pp. 1209–1224.

Ross, John A., Khaled Barkaoui, and Garth Scott, "Evaluations That Consider the Cost of Educational Programs: The Contribution of High-Quality Studies," *American Journal of Evaluation*, Vol. 28, No. 4, December 2007, pp. 477–492.

Roza, Marguerite, *Educational Economics: Where Do School Funds Go?* Washington, D.C.: Urban Institute Press, 2010.

San Francisco Unified School District, "Summer Program Facility Rental Cost: Summer 2011," 2011. As of May 11, 2011:
http://www.sfusd.edu/en/assets/sfusd-staff/doing-business-with-SFUSD/files/2011%20Facility%20Rental%20Cost.pdf

Schacter, John, and Booil Jo, "Learning When School Is Not in Session: A Reading Summer Day-Camp Intervention to Improve the Achievement of Exiting First-Grade Students Who Are Economically Disadvantaged," *Journal of Research in Reading*, Vol. 28, No. 2, 2005, pp. 158–169.

Schendel, Joel D., and Joseph D. Hagman, "On Sustaining Procedural Skills over a Prolonged Retention Interval," *Journal of Applied Psychology*, Vol. 67, No. 5, October 1982, pp. 605–610.

Schendel, J. D., J. L. Shields, and M. S. Katz, *Retention of Motor Skills: Review*, Alexandria, Va.: U.S. Army Research Institute for the Behavioral and Social Sciences, Technical Report 313, 1978.

Sherman, Rachel H., Sharon G. Deich, and Barbara Hanson Langford, *Creating Dedicated Local and State Revenue Sources for Youth Programs*, Washington, D.C.: The Finance Project, January 2007.

Shields, Joyce L., Stephen L. Goldberg, and J. D. Dressel, *Retention of Basic Soldiering Skills*, Alexandria, Va.: U.S. Army Research Institute of Behavioral and Social Sciences, Report 1225, 1979.

Silva, Elena, *On the Clock: Rethinking the Way Schools Use Time*, Washington, D.C.: Education Sector, January 2007. As of April 22, 2011:
http://www.educationsector.org/usr_doc/OntheClock.pdf

Taylor, Lori L., Mark C. Glander, William J. Fowler, Jr., and Frank Johnson, *Documentation for the NCES Comparable Wage Index Data Files, 2005*, Washington, D.C.: National Center for Education Statistics, EFSC 2007-397, August 2007.

U.S. Department of Education, "The Nation's Report Card," homepage, undated. As of June 29, 2010:
http://nationsreportcard.gov

———, *Improving Basic Programs Operated by Local Educational Agencies* (Title I, Part A), 2011. As of January 3, 2011:
http://www2.ed.gov/programs/titleiparta

Von Hippel, Paul T., Brian Powell, Douglas B. Downey, and Nicholas J. Rowland, "The Effect of School on Overweight in Childhood: Gain in Body Mass Index During the School Year and During Summer Vacation," *American Journal of Public Health*, Vol. 97, No. 4, April 2007, pp. 696–702.

Walberg, Herbert J., "Synthesis of Research on Time and Learning," *Educational Leadership*, Vol. 45, No. 6, March 1988, pp. 76–85.

Weiss, Heather B., Priscilla M. D. Little, Suzanne M. Bouffard, Sarah N. Deschenes, and Helen Janc Malone, *The Federal Role in Out-of-School Learning: After-School, Summer Learning, and Family Involvement as Critical Learning Supports*, Cambridge, Mass.: Harvard Family Research Project, February 2009.

White House, Office of Social Innovation and Civic Participation, "2010 National Summer Learning," July 8, 2010. As of April 22, 2011:
http://www.whitehouse.gov/blog/2010/07/08/2010-national-summer-learning

Winship, Scott, Matissa Hollister, Joel Howich, Pat Sharkey, and Christopher Wimer, *Promoting Education Achievement and Opportunity Through Summer Scholarships*, Washington, D.C.: New Vision and Center for American Progress, 2005.

Wiseman, Alexander W., and David P. Baker, "The American Summer-Learning Gap from an International Perspective," in Geoffrey D. Borman and Matthew Boulay, eds., *Summer Learning: Research, Policies, and Programs*, Mahwah, N.J.: Lawrence Erlbaum, 2004, pp. 53–69.